Kathy studied art at The Art Institute of Chicago and English literature at UCLA. She traveled the world with her first husband and his band, and again with her second husband, a psychoanalyst and writer. These travels inspired her love of music, history, food, and languages.

Binnie studied fine arts at Brooklyn College, where she discovered her passion for photography. Kathy and Binnie met at their daughters' preschool. Widowed within a year of each other, they decided to cohabitate, create and travel about once again. So, when life handed them lemons, they made lemon marmalade.

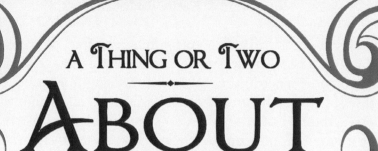

# A THING OR TWO
## ABOUT FRUIT

WRITTEN BY
### KATHY RODMAN

PHOTOGRAPHY BY
### BINNIE J. BELL

AUST'N MACAULEY PUBLISHERS™
LONDON • CAMBRIDGE • NEW YORK • SHARJAH

# Copyright © Kathy Rodman (2021)

**Ordering Information**
Quantity sales: Special discounts are available on quantity purchases by corporations, associations, and others. For details, contact the publisher at the address below.

**Publisher's Cataloging-in-Publication data**
Rodman, Kathy
A Thing or Two About Fruit

ISBN 9781645362098 (Paperback)
ISBN 9781645362081 (Hardback)
ISBN 9781645368489 (ePub e-book)

Library of Congress Control Number: 2020909699

www.austinmacauley.com/us

First Published (2021)
Austin Macauley Publishers LLC
40 Wall Street, 33rd Floor, Suite 3302
New York, NY 10005
USA

mail-usa@austinmacauley.com
+1 (646) 5125767

This book is dedicated to our children: Greg, Christian, Angela, David, Sarah, Elizabeth, and Nick for encouraging us along the way.

Heartfelt thanks to my late parents, Bill and Anne, for laughing at the stories and encouraging me to find more. Liberty, muse-extraordinaire, read many drafts and offered excellent critiques. Sid and Michele warmly hosted us in New Mexico and helped us hunt for blackcurrants. Karen and Vahan let us have our way in their orchard. The peaceful retreats on Greg and Stella's perch above Santa Barbara and weeks at Brenda's beach house provided endless inspiration. Nick Newton found Mucha's 'Fruit' and designed a perfect template for our work. Cellin Gluck, a complete stranger, invited us home to see his gooseberries.

We are forever grateful to the staff at the Getty Research Institute who motivated us early on by granting us Stack Reader privileges. The Roman Herb Garden at the Getty Villa shared its spectacular species of Mediterranean fruiting trees. Frank McDonough at the Los Angeles Arboretum returned every call and offered sound consul. Descanso Gardens provided endless photo opportunities. A botanist at the Chicago Botanic Gardens kept us current as to blackcurrants' progress. Bonnie Baraabas introduced us to Norman Beard, a rare fruit grower in Goleta. Cheers to all of the above and lastly, to Norman who drove us around his groves and delighted us with his wealth of fruit knowledge.

# Table of Contents

# Introduction

A ruby red fruit cured a demon of her child-eating habit; a purple fruit whose flower turned in upon itself sparked the third Punic War; a voluptuous yellow citrus offered antidotes to Roman poisons. Never judge a fruit by its color.

Twelve thousand years ago, people all over Earth took up farming and the fruits of their labor inspired mirth, myth, and madness as they made their way around the world with early travelers. People happily transformed their new fruits into medicine, religious symbols, trophies, and proxies for themselves in sacrifices to their gods.

Blame this book on tiny red currants. Those unfamiliar shiny orbs captivated me as they jumped into my market basket one summer morning and challenged me to make something out of them. I discovered red currants' extraordinary history, and that they created the jelly of French kings and queens. A hunger to preserve fruits and unearth their past launched this journey.

Ladies of Louis XIV's court bit lemons to redden their lips and Victorian women brightened their eyes with its juice. Greeks ate figs to increase their male potency but other cultures fancied strawberry as an aphrodisiac. Native Americans brewed blueberry tea to tranquilize women during childbirth and records show that early settlers followed their example.

Encounter fruits that repelled the evil eye, dispelled sadness, called forth spirits, drove men mad, and made women more seductive. Discover, if you can, the REAL fruit of temptation...

## Goblin Market
## Christina Rossetti


Morning and evening
Maids heard the goblins cry:
"Come buy our orchard fruits,
Come buy, come buy:
Apples and quinces,
Lemons and oranges,
Plump unpeck'd cherries,
Melons and raspberries,
Bloom-down-cheek'd peaches,
Swart-headed mulberries,
Wild free-born cranberries,
Crab-apples, dewberries,
Pine-apples, blackberries,
Apricots, strawberries;
All ripe together
In summer weather,
Morns that pass by,
Fair eves that fly;
Come buy, come buy:
Our grapes fresh from the vine,
Pomegranates full and fine,
Dates and sharp bullaces,
Rare pears and greengages,
Damsons and bilberries,
Taste them and try:
Currants and gooseberries,
Bright-fire-like barberries,
Figs to fill your mouth,
Citrons from the South,
Sweet to tongue and sound to eye;
Come buy, come buy."

# Fig
## Ficus Carica

Cato pled his case for conquering Carthage by promising figs as part of his victory. He made his point with the Roman Senate when he shook one of their juicy figs from the skirts of his toga and the Third Punic War began.

This fruit fed huge armies when other foods failed and news of places with great fig plantations often brought long wars upon those countries.

Pliny the Elder, a philosopher, noted figs made the elderly look younger with fewer wrinkles. Romans boiled figs in honey to create defritum, their fruit preservative. Defritum is believed to be the predecessor of balsamic vinegar.

Greeks alleged this fruit increased fertility and awarded dried figs to the winners of the first Olympics in 776 BC.

Fig trees symbolized peace and plenty to ancient Jews and eternal life to the Hindus. Muhammad's followers called fig the Tree of Heaven.

Buddha achieved enlightenment while meditating for six years beneath the Bodhi Tree, a 2,500-year-old fig tree that still grows in Bodh, India.

Rabbi Nehemiah, a wandering 17th-century intellectual, claimed fig was the Fruit of Temptation that brought about Adam and Eve's ruin. It is the first fruit cited in the Bible.

Birds and mammals ate figs and scattered their seeds to faraway places. This is believed to be the first fruit dried and stored by man. Fig is a flower turned in on itself and its actual fruits are the seeds.

*"That God-given inheritance of our mother country, darling of my heart, a dried fig."*
—Alexis of Thuria

# Peach
## Prunes Persia

Wizards preceded Chinese emperors when they traveled about, shooting arrows from peach-wood bows to protect their sovereigns from evil forces. Peach pits were strung around babies' ankles to bind them to life, and feverous people were struck with its branches to banish spirits of disease.

Peach was considered the strongest tree because it blossomed before its leaves sprouted.

Peaches traveled the Silk Road to Persia in 1,500 BC. Romans later brought Persian Peach trees home after they conquered that country. They sold them for the modern equivalent of $4.50 apiece and poached them in olive oil and cumin.

King John was said to have died from eating too many peaches in 1216 and the English didn't cultivate the fruit for hundreds of years until the reign of Elizabeth I.

The Peach Tree War began when a farmer killed a Native American woman for stealing a peach in 1655. Local Indians, fueled by a decade of abuse, retaliated by attacking the settlers' homes in New Amsterdam, on what is now the tip of Manhattan.

George Washington espaliered peach trees on his walls, and Thomas Jefferson brandied this fruit.

Samuel Rump, a Georgia farmer, named his cultivated peach after his wife, Elberta. He designed an icebox on wheels that enabled six crates of peaches to be shipped to New York markets, where his Elbertas were a hit.

*"The ripest peach is highest on the tree—And so her love, beyond the reach of me, is dearest in my sight."*
—James Whitcomb Riley

# Olive
## Olea Europaea

Zeus promised the city of Attica to the god or goddess who created the most useful invention. Athena's gift of olives, used for food and medicine, was chosen as a more peaceful invention than Poseidon's horse, a vehicle of war. Attica became Athens, and Athena planted the first olive tree on a hill that became the Acropolis. Legend claims her tree grows there today and that all olive trees come from it.

Olive trees were cultivated in Crete around 3,000 BC, and are believed to have been the source of the Minoan Kingdom's great wealth.

Olive oil was created to preserve Grecian olives, their main source of fat. Olives were gathered before ripening and soaked in water and wood ash. To speed things up, they slit the olives, allowing oil to seep out and better protect them.

This oil became essential to ancient Greeks, who used it for lighting, food, and medicinal purposes. Women used it as an after-bath moisturizer and exfoliated their faces with stone-ground olives.

The first Olympians lubricated their bodies with olive oil and competed in the nude. The contests were for men only. According to the legal code of that time, any woman found at the site during the games would be thrown off a nearby mountain.

Jewish kings were anointed with olive oil and Christians adopted that practice for baptisms. Muhammad claimed olive oil cured 70 diseases and advised his followers to consume it.

Van Gogh painted many of his olive trees during the last year of his life when he was allowed to venture outside the walls of his asylum in Saint-Remy in 1889.

*"The blessed tree nourishes people*
*And Zeus and Athena guard it with sleepless eyes*
*The gray-leafed tree that never dies."*
—Sophocles

## Rose
## Rosa

Rose petals rained down upon triumphant soldiers when they returned to Rome. The wealthy sprinkled guests with rosewater and served them rose-scented wine in rose-draped halls. Rose petals rouged the cheeks of prosperous women and prostitutes who charred the petals to darken their eyes.

Rose hips were an ancient food source in winter throughout America's Northern Hemisphere. Native Americans brewed this fruit into teas, cooked it into stews, and ate it raw when food was scarce.

Roses symbolized the *Cup of Life* to Buddhists and the *Virgin's Flower* to early Christians. In the War of Roses, the Yorks of the white rose fought the Lancasters of the red rose for England's 15th-century throne.

The Holy Spirit's descent from heaven in flames is depicted every year on Pentecost when rose petals shower down on parishioners inside the Pantheon.

Roses were in such high demand that 17th-century royalty used them as money.

Empress Josephine desired every rose species in existence for her gardens. To that end, Napoleon ordered his navy to seize all rose seeds and plants when they searched ships at sea.

Allied governments promoted rose cultivation in victory gardens because the hip's seeds are packed with vitamin C.

The Thousand-Year Rose, the world's oldest living rose bush, flourishes alongside what is left of Germany's Hildesheim Cathedral after the Allies bombed it. Charlemagne's son, Louis the Pious, is believed to have built that church after he received a sign from the Virgin Mary.

*"But he who dares not grasp the thorn*
*Should never crave the rose."*
—Anne Bronte

## Prickly Pear
## Opuntia

An ancient god commanded the Aztecs to find an eagle devouring a snake, perched upon a prickly pear cactus growing on a rock in a lake. Centuries later, they came upon that specter in swampy Lake Texcoco and watched as the rock grew into an island. They settled there and built Tenochtitlan in what is now Mexico City.

Native Americans assumed they shared the same essence as plants. When Navajos harvested this fruit, they plucked a hair from their heads as a sign of respect. They removed the spines by rolling the pears in the sand or singeing them in hot ash.

Nopales, prickly pear's pads, were used as canteens and to treat burns. Mexicans have cherished this vegetable since ancient times. Cabeza de Vaca, a Spanish shipwrecked explorer, spent almost ten years wandering the land he was sent to colonize. In the Gulf of modern-day Texas, natives offered him gifts of prickly pear or tuna. Spaniards brought prickly pears home and spread them around the Mediterranean.

This cactus is the origin of the Israeli word Sabra, which describes a Jewish person born in Israel with a tough skin and a soft interior. In Arabic, it is Subbar, which means patience, and represents the Palestinian struggle for freedom. It is also known as Handala, their cartoon character that won't show its face until it returns home.

An eight-mile curtain of prickly pear cactus was planted along the Guantanamo Bay Naval Base in 1961 to discourage Cubans from fleeing to the US.

Prickly Pear is one of a few plants that are both a fruit and a vegetable.

*"The prickly pear is now in full blume and forms*
*One of the beauties as well as the greatest pests of the plains."*
—Meriwether Lewis

# Elderberry
## Sambucus

"Old girl, give me some of thy wood and I will give thee some of mine when I grow into a tree," woodsmen implored the Elder Mother. Hyldemoer guarded elder trees and cursed people who rudely took her wood. She haunted babies in cribs of elder and gave them no peace until they were lifted out.

Folks refused to burn this wood for centuries for fear the devil would sit atop their chimneys but their lore suggested standing beneath its trees on Summer Solstice to see the elf-king and fairies on their way to Midsummer Night feasts.

Elderberry blossoms improved Egyptian complexions seven thousand years ago, and its berries dyed the hair of ancient Romans. Pliny noted elder wood created Rome's shrillest pipes, the most sonorous horns, as well as whistles, popguns, and peashooters.

Hippocrates declared Elder nature's medicine chest, and the 17th-century Anatomie of the Elder contended all parts of the tree, from bark to berry, offered cures for everything from toothache to plague.

Elder became a symbol of sorrow and death when Christians spread rumors that the Savior's cross was made of elder wood and that Judas hung himself from its tree.

Medieval Vampires were obsessive-compulsive counters. People piled mounds of elderberries on their windowsills to keep them busy until dawn.

Victorian women mixed warm elderberry juice with ash to create their mascara.

Warm elderberry wine was sold on wintery streets in London to cheer weary travelers until a hundred years ago.

*"Elder be ye Lady's tree, burn it not or cursed ye'll be."*
—A rhyme from the Wiccan Rede

# Mango
## Mangifera Indica

Shiva's son, Kartikeya, was strong and beautiful and rode a swift peacock. Ganesh, his other son, had the head of an elephant, stubby legs, and rode a mouse. A visiting sage promised to award the Mango of Wisdom to the boy who circled the world three times and returned first. Kartikeya orbited the planet quickly and came home to find the mango in his brother's hands. Ganesh had declared his parents his world and circled them three times. Lord Ganesh holds a mango as a symbol of attainment.

Buddha promised he would perform a miracle under a mango tree beneath a full moon. His detractors uprooted mango trees for miles around but on that promised night, they watched as Buddha planted a seed and a mango tree grew and flowered right before their eyes.

Mango inspired the beloved paisley design in Persia 2,000 years ago. Its fashion spread to Asia and India. During the Mughal period, paisley was carved in stone and worn by princes and holy men.

Akbar the Great united Muslims and Hindus and planted 100,000 mango trees in 16th-century India. Mango cultivation was a privilege of rajas.

On holy days, Hindu people brush their teeth with mango twigs, despite their toxicity. Mango is a relative of poison ivy and oak.

Mango chutney was highly regarded by Europeans until imported foods became available and it was relegated to colonists and the military.

Mango was the colonists' verb for pickling and all preserved fruits became mangos.

This King of Fruits has been around for 6,000 years, and is eaten more than any other fruit in the world.

*"The sheet of water is like a picturesquely painted canvas and it is surrounded by the orchards of flowered mango trees and sounded much like the screams of peacocks."*
—Valmiki

# Pomegranate
## Punica Granatum

Buddha cured the demon, Hariti, of her child-eating habit by teaching her to eat pomegranates instead. She became the protector of little children and Buddhist art depicts her nursing an infant while holding a pomegranate.

Xerxes's army carried spears with gold and silver pomegranate tips in place of points when they invaded Greece. Babylonians believed this fruit made them invincible and chewed the seeds before battles.

Roman women wore headdresses of pomegranate twigs to indicate their married status and baked its seeds with pine nuts and barley mash into the world's first fruitcakes.

Jewish tradition claims this fruit's 613 seeds correspond with the 613 commandments of the Torah. Many Jews eat pomegranates on the second night of Rosh Hashanah.

The Quran promises pomegranates are one of the rewards in Paradise. That book and the Bible describe pomegranates as a Gift from God.

The Moors brought pomegranates with them when they invaded Spain. They named their city, Granada, and this fruit became their national emblem during that occupation.

Queen Isabella held a pomegranate and declared she would take over Andalusia seed by seed when she began her campaign to drive the Moors out centuries later.

The French named their grenades after seed-scattering pomegranates, and their strongest troops who threw them became Grenadiers.

Many Jewish scholars claim that pomegranate is the Fruit of Temptation because it's been around since the beginning of time.

*"If you buy a pomegranate, buy one whose ripeness has caused it to be cleft open with a seed-revealing smile..."*
—Rumi

# Coconut
## Cocos Nucifera

One day, as a goddess bathed in a pool of eels, an eel transformed himself into a handsome young man and she took Tuna, that eel-man, as her lover. He warned her that a great storm would soon wash him up on her doorstep in his eel form and asked her when it did, to bury him and visit him often. She later watched as two shoots sprouted from his grave and grew into a pair of earth's first coconut trees. Coconut's flesh is called Tuna's Brains and Islanders claim Tuna's face is in the shell.

Coconut's resemblance to human heads impressed ancient cultures enough that they offered it instead of humans as sacrifices to their gods.

Island warriors carried swords of shark teeth and wore coconut-fiber body armor that was thickly hooded to protect their heads from stray rocks that their women, bringing up the rear, threw at the enemy.

Coconut water saved people during times of drought. Its fronds put roofs over their heads and its oil fueled their lamps and embalmed their dead.

Coconut is a fruit, a nut, and a seed, and can float thousands of miles at sea for months and grow wherever it washes ashore.

Thousands flock to southern India every summer to have coconuts smashed over their heads. They ignore health warnings and take part in this age-old ritual of prayer to their gods for health and success.

*"He who plants a coconut tree plants food and drink, vessels and clothing, a home for himself and a heritage for his children."*
—South Seas Saying

## Cherry
## Prunus Avium

The Virgin Mary longed for the cherries that hung on a high branch. Heavy with child, she asked Joseph to pick them but he refused, saying, "Let the father of thy child present thee with cherries if he will." At that, the tree bowed to Mary's hand. This tree is dedicated to the Virgin. Legend has it that four centuries earlier, a cherry tree offered Maya its fruit while she gave birth to Buddha.

General Lucullus introduced sweet and sour cherries to Rome in 74 BC, and legionaries spread them all over Europe. Their tangy taste earned them a place at the tables of noblemen but cherries didn't become popular in Northern Europe until the Middle Ages when they were cooked into marmalade.

Cherry blossoms signify the transience and beauty of life to the Japanese, who sent the US thousands of cherry trees as a gesture of friendship in 1912. Those trees flourish alongside the Potomac River today.

Japan's first kamikaze unit was called Yamazakura, or wild cherry blossom. Pilots painted the blossoms on their planes before their suicide missions. Their government supported the idea that the souls of those downed warriors were reincarnated in the blossoms.

Cherries have strong anti-inflammatory properties, and some believe that consuming 20 tart cherries a day can stave off arthritis and gout. The most popular cherry today is the Bing, which was developed in 1875 by Seth Luelling of Oregon and named for his Manchurian foreman.

*"I wish to die in spring, beneath the cherry blossoms,*
*While the springtime moon is full."*
—Saigyo

# Pear
## Pyrus

Prometheus pitied the nakedness of the humans he'd been tasked to create out of mud and asked Zeus for fire to warm them. Zeus refused to share fire with anyone other than the gods. So, Prometheus distracted him, by tossing a pear into their courtyard with the message, "For the most beautiful goddess." Pears were sacred to Hera and Aphrodite and the gods enjoyed watching them fight over it. Prometheus got away with fire in a hollowed gourd and brought it to humans.

Homer praised pears as a gift of the gods. Ancient traders treasured this fruit because of its long storage life.

Pears, one of the world's oldest cultivated fruits, originated in Asia Minor and China, where the trees were farmed over 3,000 years ago. The Chinese deemed pear a delicacy for the wealthy.

Europeans planted a pear tree for the birth of each daughter, and smoked pear leaves before Columbus brought them tobacco.

The first governor of the Massachusetts Bay Colony planted a European pear tree to help pilgrims feel at home. The Endicott tree still bears fruit and is believed to be the oldest living cultivated fruit tree in North America.

Pear Mania raged across New England when 19th-century gentlemen farmers competed to grow the best pears from European seedlings.

Apparently, pears went to Lizzy Borden's head before she gave her mother 40 whacks and her father 41. Her defense claimed she'd eaten four pears in the stifling heat of a barn loft and lost track of time. She was acquitted of both ax murders.

*"I had a little nut tree,*
*Nothing would it bear*
*But a silver nutmeg*
*And a golden pear."*
—English Nursery Rhyme

## Jalapeno
## Capsicum Annum

Sister Maria de Jesus de Agreda never left her convent in Spain but was carried in her blue robes to the American Southwest by angels during her many ecstasies years before the Conquistadors arrived. When the Spanish later reached New Mexico, a delegation of Jumanos Indians appeared at their mission and begged to be baptized. They told the incredulous friars the Lady in Blue had introduced them to the Catholic Faith. Two priests followed the Jumanos across Apache territory to their rancheria where Indians—carrying crosses and rosaries—greeted them.

Sister Maria returned from a visit in 1662 and jotted down the world's first written recipe for Chili con carne that called for javelina and jalapenos.

Jalapeno seeds spread from the rain forests of South America to those of the Caribbean and Mexico. The pepper's thick skin prevented it from drying well in the sun, so people created chipotle by smoke-drying them.

Smoking jalapeno was used as pepper spray in pre-Columbian times when Mayans burned rows of it to create smoke screens. Ancient Aztecs preserved their food in smoking jalapenos and punished naughty children by holding them over the smoke.

Ferdinand and Isabella asked Columbus to bring back black pepper. He carried jalapenos back to them instead and explained that they were a less expensive pepper. Spanish and Portuguese explorers spread jalapenos all over the world within 50 years.

Jalapeno is America's favorite pepper and the first of its kind to travel into space on a NASA shuttle.

*"You can keep your dear old Boston*
*Home of bass and cod:*
*We've opted for New Mexico and chili,*
*The fire of the Gods!"*
—Miles Standish IV

# Blueberry
## Cyanococcus

Saint Brigid begged the King of Leinster for land to build a convent. He agreed to give her as much land as her small cloak could cover and watched as her sisters held the corners of that cloak and covered many acres with it. The king built her convent and spent the rest of his life serving the poor. Brigid's convent was renowned for its delicious jam made from the local blueberries.

Native Americans created the world's first power bars when they mixed smoked blueberries with dried buffalo and fat. Packed with protein and calories, the bars commanded a high exchange rate when they bartered with fur traders.

Many tribes dried blueberries for winter and assumed the Great Spirit sent the berries to relieve their children's hunger during famines. They brewed a strong tea from its roots to tranquilize women during childbirth, and medical records confirm early colonial women adopted this tea for the same purpose.

Blueberries are one of the only natural foods that are truly blue. Its juice, boiled in milk, created the colonists' grey house paint.

During the Civil War, sardine canners in Maine switched to canning blueberry juice for Union troops. When the soldiers returned home, they craved more of that juice and blueberry's popularity grew.

Frederick Coville and Elizabeth White, a cranberry grower, produced America's first commercial blueberry crop in New Jersey in 1916, and blueberry fever soon swept the country.

*"You ought to have seen what I saw on my way To the Village, through Mortenson's pasture to-day: Blueberries as big as the end of your thumb, Real sky-blue, and heavy, and ready to drum."*
—Robert Frost

## Passion Fruit
## Passiflora Edulis

Passiflora vines climbed the cross and attached to the scars in the wood where the nails had been driven through the Savior. People of Jerusalem never recorded this miracle but it was revealed to St. Francis of Assisi during a starving vision.

Passionflower's corona evoked sun worship in Inca, Mayan, and Aztec cultures. Incas called the plant Vines of the Souls and believed the fruit's cavities housed their ancestral spirits.

Amazonians brewed the flowers into medicinal sedatives, and Iquito shamans mixed the plant's roots with ayahuasca, their mind-altering brew, to intensify their visions.

When the Spanish found this flower growing in South American jungles, they named it Passionflower after the Passion of Jesus and took it as a sign that the natives should be converted. They used this flower as a persuasion tool and insisted that every part of it referred to the crucifixion.

Native converts adapted their mythology onto the flower, as the Mexicans transformed their goddess, Tonantzin, into the Virgin of Guadeloupe. This allowed them to worship the way they always had without suffering conqueror abuse.

Dr. Monardes documented passionflowers' medicinal uses of indigenous Peruvians in 1569. He carried the plant home to Spain and it quickly spread all over the Old World, where its leaves became a favorite calming tea.

John Muir, hungry from his 1000-mile walk to Florida after the Civil War, tasted the fruit and wrote, "Passion fruit is the most delicious fruit I have ever eaten."

*"To Dorothea, still in that time of youth when the eyes with their long full lashes look out after their rain of tears unsoiled and unwearied as a freshly opened passion-flower..."*
—George Eliot

# Quince
## Cydonia Oblonga

Paris, the Trojan prince and most handsome man of his day was tasked to select the most beautiful goddess. Aphrodite assured him that if he chose her, he could have Helen of Troy, Earth's most beautiful woman. Paris awarded Aphrodite the prized Golden Apple and spirited Helen away from her king. Hers was the face that launched a thousand ships and started the Trojan War.

Aphrodite is often portrayed with a quince in her right hand. Quince was the Golden Apple of mythology and references to apples were actually allusions to quince.

Many historians believe Eve's Fruit of Temptation was a quince. Mesopotamians spread quince around the Mediterranean where its seeds treated pneumonia and it starred in Persian cooking 2,500 years ago.

Quince became the ancestor of all marmalades and jams when ancient Romans cooked and preserved it in honey. Athenians tossed quinces into bridal chariots and Romans served it at wedding feasts. Brides in both places nibbled this fruit to perfume their kisses before they wed.

Quince arrived in Britain via Portugal as marmalade. In Medieval Times, it was eaten as protection against the Black Death.

Joan of Arc alleged that quince jam filled her with courage and consumed it before every battle. Mary, Queen of Scots, ate it to cure her seasickness.

Quince seeds were soaked in alcohol and oil to create Bandoline, a popular French hair gel that held 19th-century ladies' curled bangs to their foreheads.

Quince became a forgotten fruit in the last century but is now enjoying a culinary comeback.

*"They dined on mince, and slices of quince, which they ate with a runcible spoon: And hand in hand, on the edge of the sand, they danced by the light of the moon, the moon..."*
—Edward Lear

# Cucumber
## Cucumis Sativus

Kappa, monkey-like magical creatures, lived in Japanese rivers and lakes. They drank the blood of humans but loved to eat cucumbers. Ancient families engraved their names on this fruit and threw it into the kappa's watery homes to appease their blood lust.

A poem from Mesopotamia, The Epic of Gilgamesh, is considered to be the world's first great work of literature. If legends of the demi-god King of Ur are true, super-human Gilgamesh feasted on wild cucumbers the story described people eating 4,000 years ago.

Cleopatra credited her health and beauty to the pickles in her diet. Julius Caesar and Napoleon both believed cucumber pickles were invigorating and served them to their troops.

Emperor Tiberius had cucumbers on his table every day of the year in the first century AD. According to Pliny, "He had raised beds made in frames upon wheels," which people moved in and out of the sun. Before the Empire fell, cucumbers were popular amongst Roman women who strung them around their waists to induce pregnancy.

The English long believed that the fruit's inherent coldness brought about death but Thomas Hill, the author of England's first book on gardening, prescribed laying ailing infants on beds of cucumbers to absorb their fevers.

During World War II, forty percent of America's pickles went into the Armed Forces' ration kits.

If you point your finger at an Italian cucumber before harvest, it may stop growing. To assure a good cucumber crop, plant them on Holy Saturday.

*"Mellowing, like some old cucumber*
*That curves and fattens on its bed,*
*From his own vats, right jolly fare,*
*Full thirty suns mine host hath fed."*
—Tennyson

# Blackcurrant
## Ribes Nigrum

Felix Kir, a French priest and resistance fighter, helped free 5,000 prisoners of war from the Longvic camp. The Nazis condemned him to death but he survived the war to be knighted and elected mayor of Dijon. Father Felix made up for the lack of his area's famous Burgundy wines that the Germans had looted by serving blackcurrant liquor in white wine to visiting dignitaries. His Kir Cocktail became an international sensation.

Blackcurrants originated in northern and central areas of Europe and Siberia and later showed up in early European herbals as Quinsy Berry because it treated quinsy, a dangerous tonsil infection. French monks created Crème de Cassis by steeping blackcurrants in casks of alcohol to cure jaundice.

Folklore considered blackcurrant to be one of the angelic fragrances. Feasting on this currant is encouraged for anyone on a spiritual quest because it is said to open the third eye to the future.

The British Ministry provided blackcurrant syrup to children during World War II to prevent scurvy.

Blackcurrants became Forbidden Fruits in 1911 because it carried white pine blister rust and threatened the logging industry. New cultivars now resist that disease and blackcurrants are making a comeback.

Blackcurrant blossoms are cultivated in Burgundy for perfumes and are an essential essence in Chanel No. 5.

*"My first is snapping, snarling, growling,*
*My second's industrious, romping, and prowling.*
*Higgledy-piggledy Here we lie,*
*Picked and plucked, and put in a pie."*
—Mother Goose

## Strawberry
## Fragaria

A man grabbed a vine and swung himself off the edge of a cliff to escape the jaws of a ferocious tiger. As he dangled there, he saw mice chewing on his vine and more tigers below. Contemplating his imminent demise, he plucked a wild strawberry from the cliff's wall and put it in his mouth. He hadn't realized how sweet a strawberry could taste until that moment.

Strawberry was a symbol of Venus to ancient Romans, who were certain it was a powerful aphrodisiac.

Pale skin was a symbol of beauty amongst wealthy medieval Europeans. Ladies endured bloodlettings for a ghostlike pallor and blushed their cheeks with strawberry juice.

The Senecas assumed the berries grew along the pathway to heaven and considered them Gifts of Creation because they were the first fruit to ripen. Many tribes baked strawberry cornmeal bread long before the pilgrims came ashore and turned it into shortcake.

Today's strawberries are a cross between the wild ones of North and South America. European explorers took them home and cultivated them at the end of the Renaissance.

Madame Tallien, a beauty at Napoleon's court, was known to bathe in 22 pounds of fresh strawberry juice.

California produces so many strawberries that if its yearly crop were laid out, berry to berry, they would wrap around the earth 15 times.

Strawberries are not true berries because there are no seeds inside this fruit. In a group all their own, strawberry's nearly 200 seeds are on the outside and each one is a separate fruit.

*"Doubtless God could have made a better berry, but doubtless God never did."*
—Dr. William Butler

## Citron
## Citrus Medica

Poisons served up at Roman dinners were a common occurrence and an easy way to get rid of enemies and annoying family members. Canidia, one of a famous trio of professional women assassins, preferred poison of hemlock in honey. Pliny the Elder prescribed citron pulp mixed with wine as its antidote.

Privileged Romans cherished citron because it was rare and prized for its healing powers. They enjoyed citron sauce over peacock tongue.

Etrog, citron's Hebrew name, is mentioned in the Torah and a feature in annual Sukkot Festivals. Scholars supposed citron was Eden's Forbidden Fruit that was cited in the Feast of Tabernacles. Women nibbled this fruit to conceive children and to ease their labor pains. Jewish communities planted citron around the Mediterranean as they migrated there during the Diaspora. They carried its seeds with them when they returned to Palestine centuries later.

Muhammad alleged citron strengthened the heart and dispelled sadness, and was best taken ten minutes after eating.

When citron showed up in China, a freak form developed and the fruit separated into five or more lobes that resembled fingers on a hand. Buddha's Hand was placed on altars as a symbol of happiness. Artists carved this fruit in ivory and jade and painted it on 10th-century wood panels.

Citron is deemed the male ancestor and purest of all citrus fruits because it self-pollinates.

*"Citron is like a true believer: good to taste and good to smell."*
—Muhammad

## Red Currants
## Ribes Sanguineum

Vikings claimed they discovered North America and named it Vinland in 1,000 AD. Archaeologists found remains of their villages on the tip of Newfoundland in 1960. Those ruins confirmed the fact that Vikings were the first Europeans to reach the New World 500 years before Columbus.

A Norse saga explains the name, Vinland, derived from the profusion of vinbar, or red currants, that they found growing in the new land. Scandinavians farmed and fermented this wine berry since Early Times.

Russians cultivated red currants in their ninth-century monastic gardens to create their famous wine. Many preferred currant to grape wines. Pushkin wrote of fair maidens who were instructed to tempt a young gallant with dance and song and to pelt him with red currants upon his approach.

The most famous red currant dish is a French seedless jelly, which required its minuscule seeds to be removed from the berries by epepineuses, or she-seed-removers, with a goose feather quill, without damaging the shape of the tiny fruit. This jelly, Bar-le-Duc, was documented in 1344.

Before the Revolution, jelly makers in that area produced up to 100,000 pounds of the jelly yearly. That market declined when the aristocracy who favored it was beheaded.

Bar-le-Duc Jelly remains the most expensive jelly in the world. Mary Queen of Scots exclaimed, upon tasting this jelly, Un rayon de solei un pot!

*"Here the currants red and white*
*In yon green bush at her sight*
*Peep through their shady leaves, and cry*
*Come eat me, as she passes by."*
—Robert Heath

# Raspberry
## Rubus Idaeus

The Raspberry King, a fairy who reigned over Scandinavian berry bushes for millennia, was a tiny old man. He donned a white jacket and red hat whenever he left the bushes and limped about. Compelled to spend a week every hundred years as a worm, the king showed his gratitude to anyone who helped him while in his insect form.

Prehistoric people are believed to have carried Himalayan raspberries across the Bering Land Bridge to America, where they found blackberries growing wild.

Chippewa and Ojibwa People called July the time of their Raspberry Moon and dried this fruit in the sun to preserve it for winter. Many tribes brewed its leaves into teas to relieve morning sickness.

Germans tamed bewitched horses by lashing raspberry twigs to their bodies. Filipinos hung the twigs outside their homes to protect themselves from wandering spirits.

Raspberries were a symbol of kindness in Christian art and its juice was used as a pigment in their illuminated manuscripts. Medieval ladies rouged their cheeks and lips with its juice.

Blowing a raspberry, a loud, spluttering noise made with the lips and tongue, has been an expression of contempt for almost a hundred years.

Judge Logan of Santa Cruz discovered that one of his garden raspberries got together with a wild blackberry outside his fence in 1881. That union created the loganberry.

Each raspberry consists of about a hundred tiny fruits, or drupelets, which contain one seed.

*"Oh, but it's hard, cruel and cold*
*Searching Cardrona for nuggets of gold*
*An ounce to the bucket and we'll all sell our souls*
*For a taste of the Gin and Raspberry."*
—1860s New Zealand Folk Song

# Lemon
## Citrus X Limon

Mediums of old employed lemons to cleanse the energy of rooms before their séances. The fruit's odor repelled unwanted souls and closed the doors to the spirit world when sessions were over. Wands of lemon tree wood are often used to draw protective spirit guides to those who are developing their psychic gifts and are most powerful during a full moon.

Lemons were once rare in Europe and only available to the wealthy. Elizabeth I favored her mead flavored with lemon zest, and jugs of it went with her wherever she traveled.

The first records of lemon juice are from the Jewish communities in Cairo where they bottled qatarmizat in the 10th century.

The Compagnie de Limonadiers was granted a monopoly to sell lemonade sweetened with honey in France 600 years later. Vendors carried it on their backs and sold cups to thirsty Parisians.

Ladies of Louis XIV's court bit lemon wedges to redden their lips. Victorian women brightened their eyes with its juice and drank it with vinegar to lighten their skin.

Many Spaniards, who scattered lemon seeds around the New World, as they conquered and converted it, died from scurvy. They had no clue that lemons offered its cure for hundreds of years.

Stonewall Jackson reportedly sucked on lemons as he sat atop his horse, Little Sorrel, during Civil War battles.

*"Do you know the land where the lemon-trees grow,*
*In darkened leaves the gold-oranges glow,*
*A soft wind blows from the pure blue sky,*
*The myrtle stands mute, and the bay tree high?*
*Do you know it well?"*
— Goethe

## Grape
### Vitis Vinifera

Dionysus created wine in Greece and spread the art of grape viticulture. Most gods were worshipped in temples but Dionysus was revered in nature. He wandered forests, accompanied by Maenads, women high on wine, draped in fawn skins and sporting pinecone-tipped staffs. Rome adopted Dionysus and named him Bacchus. Romans improved cultivation and perfected the art of winemaking. They believed wine was a daily necessity for everyone, and to ensure a steady supply, grape-farming spread to every corner of their Empire. Their wine merchants traded with tribes in Gaul and Germania and brought their influences along long before their armies arrived.

Ancient philosophers agreed that wine banished pain by cheering the soul but could also make a man mad. They claimed wine's first toast went to the goddess of fruit and to Dionysus; the second to Aphrodite and again to Dionysus but the third toast went to violence and ruin.

Moses sent spies ahead to the Promised Land and they returned, dragging a massive cluster of grapes.

Rabbi Meir, a 13th-century Israeli sage, claimed Eden's Forbidden Fruit was grape made into wine. The Talmud states that, "Only where there is no wine are drugs required." Christians embraced wine as their symbol of Christ's blood.

Two jars of dried grapes, or raisins, once bought a slave in ancient Rome. Raisins traveled the Silk Road, across the seas, to the North Pole, and into outer space with astronaut Scott Carpenter.

*"The sun, with all those planets revolving around it and dependent upon it, can still ripen a bunch of grapes as if it had nothing else in the universe to do."*
—Galileo

## Gooseberry
### Ribes Uva-Crispa

Gooseberry Warriors, a cigar-smoking gang of women, were hired
by Indian farmers to protect their crops from gooseberry thieves.
The warriors roughed up crooks twice their size by pulling on their
hair and spitting into their mouths. When urban sprawl overcame
gooseberry farms, the ladies went back to selling produce in
marketplaces where nobody dared barter with them.

Ancient people believed fairies hid from danger in gooseberry
bushes. When children asked where babies came from, they were
often told that they were found under these bushes.

To remove a sty on an eyelid, Irish lore suggests one must pluck ten
gooseberry thorns, throw one away and point nine at the eye three
times before sunset, while reciting, "In the name of the Father, and
the Son, and the Holy Ghost. Amen."

Tudors and Elizabethans stuffed their geese with gooseberries
and enjoyed fooles of the berries mixed with custard and cream.
Gooseberries were popular unless you happened to be an unwanted
third person, or a Gooseberry, at a lover's meeting.

A gooseberry craze struck England and America in 1800. Gardeners
competed to grow the berry beyond its grape size to that of a plum.
Media of the day reported on their every move as England and
America traded gooseberries. American gooseberries carried blister
rust to Britain and temporarily wiped out most of their crops in 1905.
England's oldest-surviving gooseberry club has met every August for
200 years. A whopping 2.27-ounce berry broke the world record in
2013.

*"What though the Deer bound sportively along O'er springy turf, the
Park's elastic vest? Give them their honors due —But Gooseberry pie is
the best!"*
—Robert Southey

## Banana
### Musa Acuminata

Menehunes, magical tiny people, lived in Hawaiian forests long before Polynesians arrived in banana-filled canoes. Expert archers, they were known to pierce the hearts of angry people to ignite feelings of love. Many believe these little people still roam the islands, eating bananas and tricking people.

Bananas were sacred to Hawaiian priests and chiefs. They shared the fruit with other men during famines but forbade women to eat them, under punishment of death, until that ban was lifted in 1819.

Ulawa people of the Solomon Islands, one of the banana's birthplaces, believed souls of their dead inhabited this fruit and didn't eat this fruit for fear of consuming an ancestor.

Quran and Hindu texts claim banana was the Forbidden Fruit.

In the New World, banana leaves shaded colonial coffee crops and the fruit fed its slaves.

Many ships that disappeared in the Caribbean during the early 1700s were carrying bananas and racing to get them to the colonies before they spoiled. When those top-heavy boats sank, only bananas were found floating on the sea.

Captains have been known to go bananas if they find bananas on their ships. They consider them bad luck and toss them overboard.

Recent boating bans by recreational fishermen include Banana Boat sunscreen and Banana Republic apparel.

Bananas are berries that grow on the world's largest herbs.

*"We'll sell you two kinds of red herring, Dark brown,*
*and ball-bearing*
*But yes, we have no bananas today*
*We have no bananas today."*
—Frank Silver & Irving Cohn

## Apricot
### Prunus Armeniaca

Hercules killed his family during a temporary bout of madness. He prayed for forgiveness when he came to his senses and was tasked with stealing apricots from Hera's garden. A hundred-headed dragon and Atlas's daughters guarded that garden. Hercules promised Atlas he would take over his job in return for Hera's apricots. When Atlas returned with the fruit, Hercules tricked him into holding up the sky for a bit and disappeared with the apricots.

Apricots traveled to Europe from Central Asia with Alexander the Great in the fourth century BC. The Roman-Persian wars were responsible for apricots' arrival in Italy 300 years later.

Romans called this first fruit of summer Precocious, and along with the Greeks, assumed its juice was the Nectar of the Gods.

Apricot kernels treated Chinese tumors in the fifth century and its oil did the same in England 1,200 years later.

Germans brought apricot trees indoors months before yuletide, and by Christmas morning, white blossoms filled their 17th-century rooms. For hundreds of years, women of the Austrian Silesia have carried blooming apricot branches to Christmas Mass.

American drivers supposed every tank that broke down during the Second World War had apricots on board and blamed this fruit for every mishap.

California's Golden Age of Apricots was a time between world wars when apricot groves blossomed across the Santa Clara Valley. That Valley of Heart's Delight became Silicon Valley during the high-tech revolution.

Dried apricots can last for several centuries without spoiling. Apollo 15 astronauts took apricot bars and a Lunar Roving Vehicle to the moon.

*"Be kind and courteous to this gentleman.*
*Hop in his walks and gambol in his eyes.*
*Feed him with apricots and dewberries..."*
—Shakespeare

# Plum
## Prunus Domestica

Thomas Horner was a steward to the Abbot of Glastonbury, who ordered him to deliver a Christmas pie to Henry the VIII. That enormous pie held deeds to many estates, gifts the Abbot hoped would deter the king from seizing Catholic properties. Along the way, Horner is believed to have put in his thumb and pulled out a plum, or the deed to Mells Manor, which he kept for himself. That property contained mines of lead or plumbum.

Plum trees blossom before snow melts and swallows return to China, where it is considered a Friend in Winter. Dried plums were eaten there to prevent hangovers.

Early noblewomen adorned their homes with the blossoms and painted the flowers on their foreheads.

The Japanese dried this fruit into Umeboshi and it became the Samurai warriors' most important field ration. They improved upon the Chinese species and plums soon became known to the world as Japanese Plums.

Native Americans made altars for their Sun Dances out of wild plum branches and employed wands of painted plum sprouts in prayer ceremonies for their sick.

English colonists carried plums with them to America, where they found wild ones growing along the east coast.

Japanese plums, introduced to America in the 19th century and European ones are the only commercially significant plums today.

*"The branches of the aspen plum to and fro they sway. How can I not think of her? But home is far away."*
— Confucius

## Blackberry
## Rubus Fruticosus

Blackberries were beautiful until Lucifer fell into their bushes when he was kicked out of heaven on the last day of September. He threatened to stomp on the bushes with his cloven hooves, spit on them and to curse anyone who ate the berries after that date.

Haraldskaer Woman was unearthed, preserved in peat, in a Danish bog in 1835. Modern forensics recently discovered the forty-year-old female was a sacrificial victim and blackberries were part of her last meal 2,500 years ago.

Irish folks used blackberry roots to make pipes and the fruit's longest shoots to secure their thatch roofs. Their sick children were passed beneath a blackberry arch three times before breakfast, while reciting, "In bramble, out cough, here I leave the whooping cough."

Medieval Christians claimed Christ's Crown of Thorns was made of its vines. They portrayed this fruit in their art as a symbol of ignorance but used its juice to make their indigo dyes.

Early American settlers found blackberries only after they cleared the forests as they headed west. The fast-growing shrubs sprang up, spread and were soon farmed.

Blackberry Truces were declared during Civil War battles to allow both sides to forage for the blackberry leaves needed to cure their dysentery.

Bees that feed on blackberry blossoms produce dark, fruity honey.

*"Life was much better when apple and blackberry were just fruits."*
—Unknown

# Almond
## Prunus Dulcis

Phyllis, a beautiful princess, was left at the altar but waited years for her betrothed to return. She eventually died of a broken heart and the gods turned her body into an almond tree as compensation for her grief. Upon her lover's return, he was shown Phyllis's flowerless tree. It burst into bloom as he wrapped his arms around it. Almonds symbolized true love inextinguishable by death.

Forests of wild almond trees grew along the Silk Road from China to the Mediterranean and surrounded ancient Jerusalem, where its blossoms were models for menorahs.

The rod of Aaron bore sweet almonds on one side and bitter ones on the other. God created this miracle to prove that if the Israelites obeyed Him, the rod would bear sweet fruit, but if they forsook Him, bitter almonds would prevail.

The Church directed medieval people to fast for a third of the year, during which time animal products were forbidden. Monks crushed almonds in boiling water to make almond milk and churned it into butter. Royal chefs created feasts of "illusion foods" of fish molded to look like venison and faux eggs which were eggshells stuffed with almond milk and saffron centers.

Almond's oval-shaped kernel inspired halos around religious figures in Renaissance art. Halo became Manorial, the Italian word for almond.

30 billion honeybees are trucked in from all over the country every year to help produce more than eighty percent of the world's almonds in California.

*"When the almond-blossom blows:*
*We shall have the word in a minor third*
*There is none but the cuckoo knows."*
—Robert Browning

## Pomelo
## Citrus Maxima

Long ago, ten suns cluttered the sky and scorched every plant on earth. People were dying until the hero, Yi, saved them by shooting down nine suns with his bow and arrows. The queen of heaven rewarded him with an elixir of immortality, which he entrusted to his beautiful wife, Chang'e. When thieves demanded she turn over that elixir, Chang'e drank it, became immortal and flew to the moon.

Every year, the Chinese offer Chang'e pomelos and moon cakes at their Harvest Festivals as they gaze at her full moon. Many wear hats of pomelo rinds to better attract her attention to their prayers.

They believe pomelo trees are sacred and bathe in its leaves to repel evil spirits after funerals.

Pomelo was nicknamed Adam's Apple by an early pilgrim to Palestine who claimed to have seen the marks of Adam's teeth in its rind. Later travelers observed the same phenomenon.

Yamabushi, Japanese ascetic hermits endowed with supernatural powers, created a famous pomelo seasoning from the fruit of sacred Mountain Hiko.

Pomelos got close to oranges in the Caribbean and created grapefruits. That 18th-century citrus was called Forbidden Fruit because of its bitterness.

Chinese farmers claimed that choosing a delicious pomelo was like finding a good wife; "It should be cute, not too big, have an oval face and a round bottom."

*"Peeling pomelo for the grandchildren let it be sweet. Ah, full of pulp, let it be sweet, not sour…"*
—Old Hainanese Folk Rhyme

# Tomato
## Solanum Lycopersicum

French Aristocrats called tomato Poison Apple because many died after eating it. The privileged dined off pewter plates with high lead content, and unbeknownst to them, tomato's acidity caused that lead to leach into their food.

A Parisian chef urged crowds of red-capped revolutionaries to consume red foods to prove their devotion to the Republic. They embraced tomato as their Fruit de Jour.

Tomato's name comes from the Spaniards' take on the Aztec word Tomatoti, which means plump thing with a navel. Cortez returned home with tomato seeds from Montezuma's garden but Europeans refused to eat it until the pizza was invented 300 years later.

Tomato is referred to in Hebrew as love apple, or Agvaniyah. Jewish society kept that word out of their Hebrew books because of its sexual connotations for many years.

Henry J. Heinz was the first businessman to produce organic food when he created ketchup that was free of artificial preservatives in 1906.

The Supreme Court ruled tomato was a vegetable to take advantage of a trade tariff in 1893. The USDA declared ketchup a vegetable to justify budget cuts in school lunch programs 100 years later.

The La Tomatina Festival hosts the world's biggest food fight. Tens of thousands show up every year in Bunol, Spain to throw tomatoes at each other. According to TomatoFestivalSpain.com, 120 tons of tomatoes are trucked in for that food fight.

*"A salad can be an anthem to joy*
*But the proof is in the tomato."*
—Mark Twain

# Huckleberry
## Vaccinium

Yakama chiefs prayed and fasted while their skilled pickers gathered huckleberry's first harvest. They held a Feast of Thanks when the pickers returned, and only when that feast was over, could everybody rush to the fields. A missionary noted that Indians preferred spending Sundays in berry meadows of Indian heaven than listening to stories of a Christian paradise.

Northwestern tribes made combs from the backbones of salmon to strip the berries off bushes. They mashed smoked berries into cakes and wrapped them in bark for storage. Huckleberry branches were their brooms.

Thoreau recorded the first written history of huckleberry picking, hoping to establish that natives did not learn how to use the berries from white people. He witnessed an army captain happen upon a large group of female natives gathering berries in what is now Massachusetts. Thoreau claimed Captain Church killed many and imprisoned 66 of them.

Huckleberry picking camps were erected in the summers of the 1930s and 40s. Native Americans camped on one side of the road in as many as 500 tipi lodges and northern Montanans camped on the other. These gatherings supplied boxcars of huckleberries and a unique opportunity for everyone to mingle.

Huckleberries grow wild from Wyoming to Alaska and have resisted the efforts of researchers and farmers to tame them.

Pennsylvania's Losh Run Box Huckleberry—a close relative and survivor of the last Ice Age—is estimated to be the oldest living thing on earth.

*"There's a berry blue and gold,*
*Autumn-ripe, its juices hold*
*Sparta's stoutness, Bethlehem's heart,*
*Asia's rancor, Athen's art."*
—Rose Terry Cooke

# Apple
## Malum

The Wizard, Merlin, tutored King Arthur in a magical apple grove, guarded by birds. Later, after Arthur drove the Saxons out of England, the mortally wounded king was taken home to Avalon, the Isle of Apples and land of fairies, where many believed he never died. Glastonbury, Avalon's supposed site, was once covered with apple orchards.

Travelers on the Silk Road helped themselves to this fruit as they passed forests of primeval crabapple trees. Those seeds that men and beasts dropped as they moved around grew into millions of apple trees throughout Asia and Europe.

Europeans called most fruits Apples until the Middle Ages when apples, as we know them, became models for Forbidden Fruits. Scholars believe the fruit of the Tree of Knowledge was not an apple, but a native fruit of the alleged Eden in Mesopotamia. The Latin word malus means evil and apple.

Applejack, fermented cider, was used as currency to pay colonial road crews. Most early farms had apple orchards whose crops went entirely into making applejack.

Johnny Appleseed, or John Chapman, devoted his life to the cultivation of cider apples. He planted many orchards along the western frontier. The FBI chopped down most of his trees during Prohibition 100 years later.

Peter Stuyvesant planted America's longest-living apple tree in his Manhattan orchard in 1647. It was still bearing fruit when a derailed train struck it in 1866.

*"Fair the gift to Merlin given,*
*Apple trees seven score and seven;*
*Equal all in age and size;*
*On a green hill-slope that lies*
*Basking in the southern sun,*
*Where bright waters simmering run."*
—John Gwenogvrn Evans

# Watermelon
## Citrullus Lanatus

A Roman governor had a watermelon thrown at him during a political debate in the fourth century BC. He placed a piece upon his head and thanked the thrower for providing him with a helmet to wear in his upcoming battle against Philip of Macedonia.

Watermelon was one of the Israelites' foods while they were in bondage in Egypt. They created wine from watermelons and stored it in earthen jars.

Jewish slaves were allotted two liters of watermelon wine a day but the best wines went to royal households and into pharaohs' funerary urns. Roadside stands offered thirsty travelers a glass or two.

When Egyptians and Israelites learned that grapes made better wine, they ate the fruit and pickled its rind.

Chinese relatives munched on watermelon seeds during vigils over their dead to prevent pregnant cats from leaping over the coffins and prompting corpses to sit up.

Africans hid watermelon seeds under their tongues when they were sold into slavery. They planted those seeds in small gardens that their American masters allotted them. Watermelon's water and sugar sustained them during long days of hard labor.

America's climate was so good for watermelons that the fruit escaped gardens into the wild and Native Americans farmed them across the country.

Mark Twain noted that to taste a watermelon "is to know what the angels eat."

*"To whom the watermelon is always purple,*
*Whose garden is wind and moon,*
*Of the two dreams, night and day,*
*What lover, what dreamer, would choose*
*The one obscured by sleep?"*
—Wallace Stevens

## Mulberry
## Morus

Pyramus and Thisbe agreed to meet beneath a mulberry tree one night in Babylon. As Thisbe waited for him, a lion startled her and she dropped her veil as she ran away. Pyramus came upon that lion shredding Thisbe's bloodied veil and assumed it had swallowed her. Overwhelmed with grief, he drove a sword through his heart. Thisbe found him near death and begged him to wait as she stabbed herself. Their blood pooled at the tree's roots and stained mulberries forever red.

Ancient Germans believed the devil used mulberry roots to polish his boots. Native Americans used mulberry as a laxative and as a cure for dysentery.

The Chinese discovered silkworms thrived on white mulberry leaves, and that their cocoons could be unwound and woven into silk. They guarded this secret for millennia until two monks smuggled silkworm eggs into Europe.

The English tried silk production but cultivated black mulberries by mistake in the 13th century. King James sent silkworm eggs and white mulberry seeds to Virginia and commanded the colonists to create his silk industry. Most people ignored that edict despite James's threat of heavy fines if they didn't comply. Their tobacco and cotton crops were doing just fine.

Thomas Jefferson named his slave quarters Mulberry Row after the many mulberry trees he planted to screen their cabins from his view. Milton's 400-year-old mulberry tree still stands in the garden of Christ's College in Cambridge.

*"With love juice staind the Mulberie, the fruit that dewes the poet's braine."*
—Matthew Roydon

## Pineapple
### Ananas Comosus

Columbus went ashore on the Caribbean island of Guadeloupe to investigate a deserted village. He discovered freshly gathered pineapples and piles of gnawed human bones in a parrot-filled jungle. Columbus called this curious new fruit Pine of the Indians, and the people of that place, Canibales.

Spanish sailors learned they were welcomed in Caribbean places when pineapples sat at the entrance to their villages. Pineapple's symbol of hospitality quickly spread from the Caribbean to Europe and back to the Americas.

Pineapples were rare and revered amongst royal gourmands. Their gardeners struggled to perfect a hothouse process to grow this fruit for almost two centuries. King Charles II posed for an official portrait when his gardener offered him England's first pineapple in 1675.

Colonial women competed to create the most extravagant pyramids of exotic fruit for their dinner parties. Only the fastest ships and best weather conditions could deliver pineapples fresh from the Caribbean. They were so dear that pineapples were often rented out for a day and sold to a wealthier hostess the next.

Pineapples became the darlings of artists and architects. Carved pineapples appeared on gateposts and door lintels. The fruit's image was woven into rugs and stenciled onto walls and chests as a universal symbol of welcome for centuries.

*"He is the very pineapple of politeness!"*
—Richard Brinsley Sheridan

## Orange
## Citrus Sinensis

The Queen of Navarre planted five orange seeds in a box in 1421. That box changed many royal hands until Francis I took it to Fontainebleau where it was cataloged as the Grand Constable, a tree with five branches. Louis XIV later helped himself to many of the royal families' finest trees when he created his Orangerie. Louis moved the Constable to Versailles, where it bore fruit until its death in 1894.

The War of the Oranges started when France and Spain invaded Portugal because it refused to end its relationship with England. Spaniards sent Portuguese oranges home to their queen in 1801.

Queen Victoria wore orange blossoms in her hair on her wedding day. Prince Albert gave Victoria a tiara of enameled orange blossoms and gold leaves, of his own design, on their anniversary. He added a green orange to it with the birth of each of their first four children.

William Wolfskill planted orange seedlings on two acres in what is now downtown Los Angeles. Many laughed at his plan to sell fruit but in a few years, he was selling oranges to Gold Rush miners for a dollar apiece.

The USDA's first botanist sent two saplings from a new Brazilian navel orange tree to Eliza Tibbets to see if the fruit would grow in Riverside, California. The trees produced huge seedless fruits that were said to outshine every other.

Millions of trees have been propagated from Eliza's mother trees, one of which bears fruit today at the corner of Magnolia and Arlington.

*"Gay go up, and gay go down, To ring the bells of London town. Oranges and lemons, Say the bells of St. Clements."*
—Tommy Thumb's Pretty Song Book

## Cranberry
## Vaccinium Macrocarpon

Long ago, fierce mastodons walked the earth and made war upon smaller animals. The Creator instructed the Lenape people to fight alongside the animals. The Ohio River Valley quickly ran thick with the animal's blood and eventually became a quagmire that swallowed those heavy mastodons. In memory of that ancient battle, the Creator created blood-red cranberries in that marshland.

Cranberry Day was the most important holiday for the Wampanoag Tribe who lived on Martha's Vineyard 12,000 years before the Mayflower dropped anchor. In the spirit of their ancestors, after the October cranberry harvest every year, they gave thanks to the Creator with song, dance, and a feast.

Squanto, an English-speaking brave, and other Wampanoags taught starving pilgrims how to harvest cranberries. Colonists discovered iron ore beneath cranberry bogs and it became the source of metal for their Revolutionary War weapons.

General Ulysses S. Grant demanded that cranberry sauce be served to his troops before the nine-month Siege of Petersburg in 1864. American troops consumed one million pounds of dehydrated cranberries every year during World War II.

Cranberries last a long time because they produce their own preservatives.

America's first harvesters discovered that by flooding bogs with water, they rose to the surface for easy picking. Growers today still test the berry's ripeness by dropping them. If they bounce, they're good to go.

Elizabeth Lee boiled her bruised berries with sugar and spices. She tried to market her sauce in 1917 but there was little interest. A few years later, she formed her own company and cranberry sauce caught on. She later merged with another company and they became Ocean Spray.

*"… as why are Strawberries sweet and Cranberries sowre, there is no reason but the wonderful work of God that made them so…"*
—John Elliot

## Pumpkin
### Cucurbita Maxima

One night in Ireland, Stingy Jack convinced the Devil to turn himself into a coin to pay for their drinks. Jack pocketed that coin next to a cross and only released the Devil on the condition that when he died, the Devil would not claim his soul. Upon his death, God would not let Jack into heaven and the Devil condemned him to roam the earth with a burning coal in a carved-out turnip. His ghostly figure was known as Jack of the Lantern.

Celtic people placed carved vegetable faces in their windows to repel wandering spirits on the last day of October, the onset of the dark half of the year and a time when ghosts had access to their world. Irish immigrants discovered pumpkins made perfect jack o' lanterns when they arrived here.

Native Americans dried strips of pumpkin and roasted them for food or wove them into mats. Pumpkin shells were their bowls and its seeds treated their kidney ailments. They introduced pumpkins to the pilgrims.

Pilgrims sliced off a pumpkin's top, filled the inside with milk, honey, and spices, and baked it in hot ashes. They used this fruit as a template for haircuts and earned themselves the nickname Pumpkin-Heads.

Columbus presented pumpkins to Europeans who considered it poor man's fare. Washington, Jefferson, and other American Colonists fed it to their pigs.

The world's largest berry, pumpkin, originated in Central America but has been growing in North America for 5,000 years.

*"For pottage and puddings and custards and pies, Our pumpkins and parsnips are common supplies: We have pumpkins at morning and pumpkins at noon, If it were not for pumpkins, we should be undoon."*
—Pilgrim Verse

# Eggplant
## Solanum Melongena

Hungry fallen angels wandered around the Dead Sea until they found eggplants. When they bit into the fruit, its pulp turned to powder, according to Milton. Eggplants grew near the site of Sodom and Gomorrah, those cities of sinners that God reduced to ashes. Scholars believe eggplant is what the Bible describes as Dead Sea Fruit.

Ancient excavated eggplant remains revealed tiny insects had invaded its flesh and caused the pulp to decay while its skin remained intact.

Married ladies of early Chinese courts stained their teeth black with eggplant skins and polished them until they sparkled like metal.

African eggplants were known as Tomatoes of the Jews of Constantinople because the Jews carried this fruit there when they were driven out of Spain.

The first European who ate a raw eggplant was said to have had an epileptic fit and rumors of that incident haunted the fruit for centuries.

Many knew this fruit as Madde Apple and the people who ate them were considered crazy.

Louis XIV promoted eggplants but his court resisted it and hoped the new coffees and chocolates would distract him.

Thomas Jefferson farmed America's first eggplants but New York's Delmonico's introduced them to a larger audience in the 1830s.

Eggplant is botanically a berry. This fruit is kin to tobacco and 20 pounds of it contain the same amount of nicotine as a cigarette.

*"Spheroid fruit, pleasing to taste,*
*Fattened by water gushing in all the gardens,*
*Glossy cupped in its petiole,*
*Ah heart of a lamb in a vulture's claws."*
—Ibn Sara

# Tobacco
## Nicotiana Rustica

Long ago, when humans and animals spoke the same language, only one tobacco plant existed. Many enjoyed its fruit until greedy geese flew south with it. They sent animals to retrieve it but the geese killed them all. A hummingbird assured the skeptical humans that, despite his tiny size, he would rescue that plant without being seen. Quick as a wink, he returned tobacco to the Cherokee people.

Native Americans blew tobacco smoke into warriors' faces before battles and over women before intercourse. Many believed exhaled smoke carried their thoughts and prayers to the spirit world.

Tobacco was praised as a wonder drug when Columbus received it in 1492. Rumors of its medicinal magic quickly spread across Europe and it was embraced as a cure-all for almost everything. Dr. Nicolas Monardes' book claimed tobacco cured cancer a century later.

Sir Walter Raleigh made smoking popular at Elizabeth I's court and convinced the queen to try it.

John Rolfe, Pocahontas' husband, exported the first Virginia tobacco to England in 1614.

Between Civil War battles, Union and Confederate soldiers enjoyed unofficial truces. They played cards together and traded coffee for Confederate tobacco until they were ordered to pick up their guns.

Tobacco fruit is a tiny capsule that contains two seeds, and it is the most grown plant in the world that is not used for food.

*"... And a seat, too, 'mongst the joys*
*Of the blest Tobacco Boys;*
*Where, though I, by sour physician,*
*Am debarr'd the full fruition*
*Of thy favors, I may catch*
*Some collateral sweets, and snatch*
*Sidelong odors, that give life*
*Like glances from a neighbor's wife..."*
—Charles Lamb

# Bibliography

**FIG**

Encyclopaedia Britannica, or Dictionary of the Arts and Sciences, 1854, Vol. 6, p.338, Edinburgh, SCT, A. Constable, A and C Black, https://books.google.com/books?id=kWxBAAAAcAAJ

Knight, Charles, The English Encyclopedia: Geography, 1854, London, UK, Vol. I, p. 889, https://biodiversitylibrary.org/item/58278#page/5/mode/1up

Pliny, the Elder, Delphi Complete Works of Pliny the Elder, 2015, Delphi Classics, Version 1, Chapter 16, https://book.google.com?book?id=OrJ0CgAAQBAJ&pg=RA4-PA11&lpg=RA4-PA11&dq=pliny+the+elder+on+figs+and+wrinkles&source=blots

Mrs. Murray-Aynsley, Symbolism of the East and West, 1900, London, UK, George Redway, Chapter VIII, www.masoniclib.com/images/images0/121467942570.pdf

Defritum, Cooks Info, https://www.cooksinfo.com/defritum

Lane, Mark, The Mystery of the Fig Tree, https://biblenumbers.files.wordpress.com/2014/07/mystery-of-the-fig-tree-v3.pdf
El-Naggar, Zaghloul, Figs Resemble the Heaven's Fruits, www.elnaggarzr.com/en/main.php?=22

Elsen, Gustavus A., 1901, The Fig Its History, Culture and Curing, Washington DC, The Government Printing Office

Silberberg, Naftali, What Sort of Fruit Tree was the Tree of Knowledge?, Chabad.org. https://www.chabad.org/parshah/article_cdo/aid/983693/jewish/What-Sort-of-Fruit-Tree-was-the-Tree of knowledge.htm

Debussche, Max, Isenmann, Paul, 1989, Fleshy Fruit Characters and the Choices of Bird and Mammal Seed Dispensers in a Mediterranean Region, Vol. 56, No. 3, p.327-338, Oikos, Hoboken, NJ, Wiley, https://www.jstor.org/stable/3565617?seq=1/subject

Agapakis, Christina, September 2010, Everything You Never Wanted to Know About Figs, The Atlantic, Boston, Mass, https://www.theatlantic.com/daily-dish/archice/2010/09/everything-you-never-wanted-to-know-about-figs/182554/

**PEACH**

Simoons, Frederick J., 1991, Food in China: A Cultural and Historical Inquiry, Boca Raton, FL, CRC Press, Taylor & Francis Group LLC, p.218, https://books.google.com/

books?id=H0JZDwAAQBAJ&pg=PA218&lpg=PA218dq=-Food+in+China:+a+cultural+and+historical+inquiry+peach&-source=blots

Dore, S.J, Henry, Kennelly, S.J. (translator), 1914, Researches into Chinese Superstitions, Shanghai, Tusewei Press, Vol. 5, p. 505, https://www.scribd.com/document/345579909/researches-in-to-chinese-superstitions-Vol-5-henry-dore
Peach Facts: Peachy Keen, All About Peaches, The Nibble, www.the nibble.com/reviews/MAIN/fruits/peach-facts.asp

The Growing World, or, Progress of Civilization, and the Wonders of Nature, Science, Literature and Art, 1881, Philadelphia, PA, W.M. Patterson & Co., p.240, https://books.google.com/books?id=uOkKAAAAYAAJ&pg=PA240&lpg=PA240&lpg=PA240d-q=the+growing+world+or,+progress+os+civilization+and_the+wonders+of+nature,+science,+literature+and+art+peaches&-source+bl&ots

The Peach Tree War, September 15, 1655, https://njcu.edu/pro-grams/jchistory/Pages/P_Pages/Peach_Tree_War_1655.html

Ten Facts About the Gardens at Mount Vernon, https://www.mount-vernon.org/the-estate-gardens-at-mount-vernon/ten-facts-about-the-gardens-at-mount-vernon/

Preet, Edythe, June 1991, Thomas Jefferson: A Gourmet in the White House, Los Angeles, California, Los Angeles Times, latimes.com/1991-06-27/food/fo_1654_1_thomas-jefferson

Woolverton, Linus Ed., 1897, Elberta Peach, Canadian Horticulture and Home Magazine, Toronto, Vol. XX, p. 447, Fruit Growers' Association of Ontario, https://www, books.google.com/books?id=OCh-JAQAAMAAJ&pg=PA447&pg=PA447&dq=Samuel+rump%27+elberta+peaches&source=bl&ots

## OLIVE

Morford, Mark P.O., Lenardon, Robert J., Sham, Michael, 2011, Contest for Athens, Classical Mythology, Ninth Edition, Oxford, Oxford University Press USA, https://global.oup.com/us/compnaion.websites/9780195397703

Firenze, Carol, 2011, Mythology 101: The Greatest Gift, https://www.oliveoilsource.com/article/mythology-101-greatest-gift

The History of the Olive, The Olive in California, Mythology, The Olive Oil Source, https://www.oliveoilsource.com/page/history-olive

Ancient Greek Food: Olives, Food Editorial.co, https://www.streetdirectory.com/food_editorials/cuisines/european_cuisine/ancient_greek_food_olives.html

Ancient Skin Care Secrets Still Used Today, YASOU, 2014, https://www.yasouskincare.com/ancient-greek-skin-care-secrets-still-used-today

Reilly, Mary, Olympic Oddities: The Surprising, Historical Highlights About Ancient Olympic Games, https://www.uc.edu/vivaspx-?id=19160

Dorfman, Marjorie, Olive Oil: A History Noble, Healthy and Slippery, www.ingestand imbibe.com/Articles/oliveOil.html

Eskew, Michaela, Olive Trees with the Alpilles in the Background: A Study of Vincent van Gogh's Doctrine of Providence, https://www. academia.edu/23545813/Olive_Trees_with_the_Alpilles_iudy_ of-Vincent_van_Gogh_s_Doctrine_of_Providence

## ROSE

Holland, Tom, 2015, Dynasty: The Rise and Fall of the House of Caesar, London, UK, Little Brown, https://google.books.com/ books?id=isbn:978-0-7481-2789-4

Brown-Ferlei, Nicola, 2014, Ancient Roman Beauties and Their Makeup Bag, https://www.italymagazine.com/featured-story/ancient-roman-beauties-and-their-makeup-bag

Native Foods – Rose hips, www.kstrom.net/isk/food/wildrose. Html

Marien, Catherine, Language of Roses and Rose Symbolism, www. lillysrosegarden.com/rose-colors-symbolism.htm/
Pentecost at the Pantheon: A Rainfall of Rose Petals, 2014, https:// italymagazine.com/news/pentecost-parthenon-rainfall-petals

Our Rose Garden, the History of Roses, University of Illinois Extension, https://extension.illinois.edu/roses/history.cfm

Silverthorne, Elizabeth, 1996, Legends and Lore of Texas Wildflowers, College Station, TX, Texas A & M University Press, https://books. google.com/books?id=isbn 0-89096-702-4

Davidson, Alan, The Oxford Companion To Food, 1999, New York, The Oxford University Press Inc., p.672

Harvey, Ian, 2017, The Rose of Hildesheim: A thousand-year old rose that's believed to be the oldest in the world, https://thevintagenews.com/2017/05/02/the-rose-of-hildesheim: a-thousand-year-rose-that's-believed-to-be-the-oldest-living-rose-in-the-world/

**PRICKLY PEAR**

Herz, Mary, 2017, The Legend of the Foundation of Tenochtitlan, The Foundation of Mexico City, Origin of Mexico's National Shield, https://www.inside-mexico.com/the-legend-of-tenochtitlan/

Dewitt, David, 2011, Southwest Table: Traditional Cuisine From Texas, New Mexico and Arizona, Guilford, CT, Lyons Press, https://books.google.com/books?isbn=1461745888

Cacti and Grasses, Cacti, Prehistory, Chimney Rock National Monument, www.chimneyrockco.org/puebloan-resources/cactigrasses/

Nopales (Cactus) Nutrition Facts, https://www.nutrition-and-you.com/nopales.html

Prickly Pear, Cactacae, https://www.texasbeyond/history.net/st.plains/nature/images/prickly.htm

Cabeza de Vaca, Alvar Nunez, 1542, Bandelier, Fanny (translator), 1905, Clear Lake, Texas, University of Houston/coursesite.uhcl.edu/HSH/Whitec/texts/Mexhip/CabezaDaVacaSictns.htm

Beinart, William, Wotshela, Luvuyo, 2003, Prickly Pear in Eastern Cape Since the 1950s – perspectives from interviews, No. 29, Environmental History, Cape Town, ZA, University of Western Cape, pp. 191-209, https://www.jstor.org/stable/41056500

Haskell, David, 2017, The Songs of Trees: Stories From nature's Great Connectors, New York, NY, Penguin, https://books.google.com/books?id=9780525427520

Cactus Curtain, Global Security.org, https://www.globalsecurity.org/military/facility/guantanamo-bay_cactus-curtain.htm

Washburn, Carolyn, 2011, Prickly Pear Cactus, Food Sense to Eating Fresh Fruits and Vegatables, Utah State University Cooperative Extension, https://digitalcommons.usu.edu/extension_curall/150/

**ELDERBERRY**

Brobst, Joyce (Ed), 2013, History and Lore of Sambucus, Herb Society of America, Kirtland, OH, www.herbsociety.org/file_download/inline/a54e481a-e368-4414-af68-2e3d42bc0bec

Freeman, Mara, Tree Lore: Elder, https://www. Druidry.org/library/trees/tree-lore-elder

King, Mike, 2014, Elderberry, A Flu Virus's Worst Nightmare, https://www.marimann.com/wp-content/uploads/2014/10/Elderberry

Knowles, George, The Elder Tree, In Worship of Trees, https://www.controverscial.com/in%20worship%of%20Trees%20-%20Elder.htm

Elderberry History and Research, https://www.360okfarms.com/portfolio/elderberry-history-and-research/

Morgenstern, Kat, Sacred Earth, Elder in Profile, www.sacredearth.com/ethnobotony/plantprofiles/elder.php

Wood, Matthew, 1997, The Book of Herbal Wisdom, Berkeley, CA, North Atlantic Books, ISBN-13: 978-1-55-643-232-3, https://ww.homeopathycenter.org/homeopathy-today/book-herbal-wisdom-matthew-wood

Hooke, Della, 2010, Trees in Anglo-Saxon England: Literature, Lore and Landscape, Woodbridge, UK, Boydell Press, p. 235, ISBN 978-1-84383-565-3, https://doi.org/10.1111/j.1468-0254.20012.00342_6.x

Montez, Madame Lola, 1858, The Arts of Beauty; Or, Secrets of A Lady's Toilet, NEW YORK, NY, Dick & Fitzgerald Publishers, eyelashesinhistory.com/19thcentury.html

**MANGO**

Pattanaik, Devdutt, 2011, 99 Thoughts on Ganesha, Mumbai, India, Jaico Publishing House, Mumbai, IN, p.29, https://books.google.com/books? Isbn=8184951523

Brown, Robert L, 1984, The Sravasti Miracles in the Art of India and Dvaravati, Archives of Asian Art, Durham, NC, Duke University Press, Vol.37, p.79-95
https://www.jstor.org/stable/20111145?seq=1#page_scan_tabs_controls

Roots of the Paisley Pattern, Paisley.org, https://www.paisley.org.uk/2013/01/roots-of-the-paisley-pattern/

Davidson, Alan, 1999, The Oxford Companion To Fruit, New York, NY, Oxford University Press Inc., p.475

Lloyd, John, Mitchinson, John, Harkin, James, Murray, Andrew, 2015, Qi: The Third Book of General Ignorance, London, UK, Faber & Faber, p.29, https://books.google.com/books?isbn=0571309003
A – Z of Homemade Chutney, Pickles and Relishes. 2014, Warwickshire, UK, Two Magpies Publishing (Author), www.twomagpiespublishing.com/book-shop/a-z-of-homemade-chutney-pickles-and-relishes/ isbn 978 1473320604,

Creed, Richard, 2010, September 5, Relative Obscurity: Variations of Antigodlin grow, Winston-Salem, NC, Winston-Salem Journal

Mango – The Ayurveda King of Fruits, VPK by Maharishi Ayurveda, https://www.mapi.com/ayurvedic-knowledge/plants-spices-and-oils/mango-the-ayurvedic-king-of-fruits.html

Scherrer, Jim, 2007, The Most Popular Fruit in the World, Puerto Vallarta, MX, Banderas News, www.banderasnews.com/0712/man-gomango.htm

**POMEGRANATE**

Stone, Damien, 2017, Pomegranate: A Global History, London, UK, Reaktion Books Ltd., https://books.google.com?-books?isbn=1780237952

Pomegranate in Ancient & Modern Greece, the delphiguide.com, https://thedelphiguide.com/pomegranate-in-ancient-modern-greece/

Small, Ernest, 2012, Top 100 Exotic Food Plants, Boca Raton, FL, CRC Press, Taylor & Francis Group, https://books.google.com/books?id=isbn-13:978-1-4398-5688-8

Rhodes, Jesse, 2010, Fruitcake101: A Concise Cultural History of This Loved and Loathed Loaf, Washington, DC, Smithsonian.com. https://www.smithsonianmag.com/arts-culture/fruitcake-101-a-concise-cultural-history-of-this-loved-and-loathed-loaf-26428035/

9 Jewish Things About Pomegranates, https://www.myjewishlearning.com/article/9-jewish-things-about-pomegranates

Zaufishan, 2012, Plants of the Quran: Pomegranate, Green PROPHET SUSTAINABLE NEWS FOR THE MIDDLE EAST, https://greenprophet.com/2012/07/plants-quron-pomegranate/

POMEGRANATE HISTORY & TIMELINE, www.foodreference.com/html/a-pomegranate-history. Html

New: French Old Guard Grenadiers – Warlord Games, www.warlordgames.com/new-french-old-guard-grenadiers/

Pomegranate: fruit of the gods, 20 August 2005, https://www.independent.co-uk/incoming/pomegranate-fruit-of-the-gods-307099.html

**COCONUT**

McCormack, Gerald, 2005, The Origin of the Coconut Palm, Cook Islands Biodiversity & Natural Heritage Articles, Rarotonga, Cook Islands, cookislands.bishopmuseum.org/showarticle.asp?id=15

Why Coconuts Are Religiously Important in Hinduism, 2017, logical-hindu.com/coconuts-religiously-important-hinduism/

Arms and Armour, web.prm.ox.ac.uk/weapons/index.php/tour-by-region/oceana/oceana/arms-and-armour-oceana-222/
COCONUT TREE, 2018, Tetiaroa Society Newsletter, https://www.Tetiarroasociety.org/island/plants/coconut-tree

Drift Seeds And Drift Fruits, Seeds That Ride The Ocean Currents, 1998, https://www.palomar.edu/users/warmstrong/p/dec.398.htm

Finnis, Alex, August 13, 2014, INDIA'S human coconut shy! Thousands ignore health warning and wait in line to have the rock hard fruit smashed over their skulls 'because it brings success,' UK, The Daily Mail.com, https://www.dailymail.co.uk/news/article-2723690/Watch-Indian-devotees-smash-coconuts-HEADS-Tamil-Nadu-ritual-plea-gods-health-success.html

**CHERRY**

Chamberlain, Alexander Francis, 1896, The Child and Childhood in Folk-Thought (The Child In Primitive Culture), New York NY, MacMillan and Co., https://archive.org/details/childchildhoodin00chamuoft/page/n6

How Products Are Made, Cherries, www.madehow.com/Volume-6/Cherries.html

Ermatinger, James W, 2015, the World of Ancient Rome: A Daily Life Encyclopedia: Santa Barbara, CA, Greenwood, p.328

Cherry/encyclopedia.com, https://www.encyclopedia.com/plants-and-animals/plants/plants/cherry

Middle Ages Food – Fruit, Cherry, www.lordsandladies.org/middle-ages-food-fruit.htm

Hodgins, Vern, 2018, Cherry blossoms symbolize beauty & transient nature of life, Peel Region Review.com, https://peelregionreview.com/cherry-blossoms-symbolize-beauty-and-transient-nature-of-life/

History of the Cherry Trees, Nation Park Services, https://www.npa.gov/subjects/cherryblossoms/history-of-the-cherry-trees.htm

Ohnuki-Tierny, Emiko, 2002, Kamikaze, Cherry Blossoms, and Nationalisms: The Militarization of Aesthetics in Japanese History, Chicago, Ill, University of Chicago Press

Adams, Mike, 2013, Miracle Cure for Gout and Arthritis Pain www.grovepharmacy.com/miracle-cure-for-gout-and-arthritis-pain-six-cherries-a-day/

Curry, Diane,2012, The Myth About the Bing Cherry, https://patch.com/california/castrovalley/bp--the-myth-about-the-bing-cherry

**PEAR**

Myths and Legends, Prometheus, mythencyclopedia.com/Pa-Pr/

Prometheus.html

Janick, Jules, The Pear in History, Literature, Popular Culture and Art, https://hort.purdue.edu/newcrop/janick-papers/pear in history.pdf

Origin, Domestication, and Dispersing of Pear, https://www.hindawi.com/journals/aag/20141/541097/

Recipe: Fresh Fruit Facts & Folklore, https://www.stemilt.com/uncategorized/fresh-fruit-facts-folklore/
The Endicott Rear Tree Today, https://inhabitat.com/americas-oldest-pear-tree-still-bearing- fruit-at-363-years/

Smith, Andrew F (ed), 2004, Oxford Encyclopedia of Food and Drink in America, New York NY, Oxford University Press, Vol. I, p.530

Eddy, Cheryl, 2015, All the Evidence Against Lizzie Borden and Why She Was Acquitted, https://gizmodo.com/all-the-evidence-against-lizzie-borden-and-why -she-was-1721936980

## JALAPENO

Preuss, Arthur (ed), 1919, Venerable Maria de Agreda's alleged Miraculous Flight to New Mexico: The Historical Interview, St. Louis, MO, The FortNightly Review, Vol. XXVI, p.116, https://books.google.com/books?id=zGFAAAAAYAAJ&pg=PA116&lpg=PA116&dq=venerable+maria+de+agreda+alleged+miraclous+flight+to+new+mexico&source=blots=53dYEDU5y9&sig=ACFU3U

Maria de Agreda – The Lady in Blue, www.mariadeagreda.info

The History of Chipotle, chipotlepeople.com?pageid=812

Vann, Mick, 2012, Chipotle Chilis: The history of chipotle chilis is rich and flavorful, https://www.austinchronicle.com/daily/food/2012-08-26/chipotle-chilis/

Kremer, William, 2015, is the chili pepper friend or foe? BBC News Magazine, https://www.bbc.com/news/magazine-34411492

Rahn, Peggy, 2019, Knight-Ridder Newpapers, https://www.chicagotribune.com/news/ct-xpm-1988-06-02-8801040275-story.html

Fresh Fruits and Vegetables in Space, https://www.nasa.gov/audience/forstudents/9-12/features/F_Fruits_and_Vegetables_Space.html

**BLUEBERRY**

Brigidine Sisters: Legend of St. Brigid's Cloak, brigadine.org.an/about-us?our patroness/legend-of-st-brigids-cloak/

St. Brigid and the Biddys, Killorglin Archive, 2014, killorglinarchives.com/st-brigid-and-the-biddys/

Swagerty, William R, 2012, Indianization of Lewis and Clark: Vol. I, Norman, OK, Oklahoma Press

A History of Blueberries, wildblueberries.net/bluehistory.html

Burnham, Emily, 2014, Ten Things You Might Not Know About Blueberries, Bangor, ME, Bangor Daily News, https://bangordailynews.com/2014/08/05/living/ten-things-you-might-not-know-about-blueberries/

Bennet, Laura Dean, 2015, It's time for blueberries, Marlinton. WV, Pocahontas Times, https://pocahontastimes.com/its-time-for-blueberries/

Blueberries Were First Sold as a Commercial Crop in 1916, 2017, AgHires, https://aghires.com/blueberries-history-agricultural-facts/

## PASSION FRUIT

Skinner, Charles M, 1915, Myths and Legends of Flowers, Trees, Fruits and Plants, In All Ages and In All Climes, Philadelphia, PA, J. B. Lippincott Company, p.211, https://books.google.com/books/about/myths_and_legends_of_Flowers_Trees_Fruit.html?id=VeYOAAAAQAJ

Passion Flower, Flower of Leo and the Sun, 2015, Lunar Home and Garden, https://lunarhomeandgarden.com/2015/07/24/passion-flower-flower-of-leo-and-the-sun

Cleversly, Keith, 2002, Passiflora spp. – Passion Flower, entheology.com/ entheology.com/plants/passiflora-passion-flower/

The Symbolism of the Passion Flower, www.paghat.com/passiflora-symbolism.html

Passionflower, www.inriodulce.com/links/passionflower.html

Muir, John, Bade, William Frederic (Ed), 1916, A Thousand-Mile Walk To The Gulf, Boston, New York, Houghton Mifflin Company, The Riverside Press, Cambridge, https://vault.sierraclub.org/john_muir_exhibit/writings/a_thousand_mile_walk_to_the_gulf/

## QUINCE

Hamilton, Edith, 1942, Mythology, Boston, MA, Little, Brown and Company, Part 4, Chapter 1, https://books.google.com/books/about/Mythology.html?id=H6c_OazhNPsC

Grieve, Margaret, 1931, A Modern Herbal, Volume 2, p. 665, San Diego, CA, Harcourt, Brace and Company, https://books.google.com/books?id=isbn-13:978-0-486-22799-3, isbn-10: 0-486-22799-5

Davidson, Alan, 1999, The Oxford Companion to Food, New York,

NY, Oxford University Press Inc, p.645

Lim, T.K., 2012, edible, Medicinal and Non-Medicinal Plants, Vol. 4, New York, NY, Springer Publishing, ISBN 978-94-007-4053-2

Strong, James, M'Clintock, John, 1891, Cyclopaedia of Biblical, Theological, and Ecclesiastical Literature, New York, NY, Harper & Brothers Publishers, Vol I, https://books.google.com.na/ books?id=xNssAAAAYAAJ&printsec-front cover&source=gbs_ge_ summary_r%cad=0#v=onepage&q&f=false

The Story of Quince, https://prospectbooks.co.uk/wp-content/uploads/2014/09/Quinces_extract.pdf

Dick, William B, 1872, Encyclopedia of Practical Receipts and Processes, Part 7, 1154, https://chestofbooks.com/reference/Encyclopedia-Of-Practical-Receipts-And-processes/Cosmetics-for-the-Skin-and-Complexion-Part-7.html

Adams, Barbara Berst, 2012, The Disappearance and Revival of Fruiting Quince, Heirloom Coordinator, https://www.heirloomgardner.com/plant-profiles/edible/fruit/fruiting-quince-zmaz12fzfis

**CUCUMBER**

Swancer, Brent, 2015, The Mysterious Kappa of Japan, https://mysteriousuniverse.org/2015/03/the-mysterious-Kappa-of-Japan

History of Cucumbers, www.vegetablefacts.net/vegetable-history/history-of-cucumbers

We're no fickle pickles when it comes to fun, 2009, Jacksonville, FL, The Florida Times-Union.com, https://www.jacksonville.com/community/shorelines/2009-05-23/story/were_no_fickle_pickles_when_it_comes_to_fun

Pruitt, Sarah, 2015, Pickles Throughout History, https://www.history.com/news/pickles-throughout-history-2

Hill, Thomas, 1558, A Most Briefe And Pleasaunte Treatise Teaching How To Dresse, Sow And Set A Garden, https://thegardentrust.blog/2015/01/03/the-first-english-books-on-gardening/

Malossini, Andrea, Masotti, Marta, (T), 2013, Italian Superstitions, https://books.google.com/books?id=3q8dv0cPHslC&pg=PT44&dg=-cucumber+
Superstitions&source

**BLACKCURRANT**

Gallia Watch, the Countdown from France has Begun, Stay au courant, Felix Kir, galliawatch.blogspot.com/2007/08/flix-kir.html

Dunn, Elizabeth G., 2015, The Kir Cocktail Is Cool Again, The Wall Street Journal, New York, NY, https://www.wsj.com/articles/the-kir-cocktail-is-cool-again-1440011729

Blackcurrant facts, SoftSchools.com/www.softschools.com/facts/plants/black_currant_facts/1565

Just The Berries, Blackcurrant, 2013, www.jtbpd.com/information.phpinformation_id=18

Bosman, Get, 2015, Crème de Cassis, Distillique,distillique.co.za/distilling-shop/articles/crème-de-cassis.html

Herbal Picnic, Guide to Herbal remedies & Magic with Practical Recipes, https://herbalpicnic.blogspot.com/2013/08/black-currant.html

Trueman, C.N., 2015, children and Rationing, The History Learning Site, https://www.historylearningsite.co.uk/world-war-two/world-war-two-in-western-europe/britains-home-front-in-world-war-two/

children-and-rationing/

McGlynn, Patricia, 2006, Welcome back blackcurrants: Forbidden fruit making a comeback in New York, Ithaca, NY, Cornell Chronicle, news.cornell.edu/stories/2006/07/welcome-back-black-currants-forbidden-fruit-making-ny-comeback

Blackcurrant, Beaune & Pays Beaunois, Office De Tourism, http://www.beaune-tourism.com/tasting/local-products/blackcurrant

**STRAWBERRY**

The Strawberry: A Zen Tale from Japan: storyarts.com/library/nutshell/stories/strawberry.html

Strawberries & More: University of Illinois Extension, https://extension.illinois.edu/strawberries/history.cfm

Grossart, Sarah, 2015, Brush Up On These 10 Facts About Blush, mentalfloss.com/article/72650/brush-these-10-facts-about-blush

Fruit in Mythology: https://www.encyclopedia.com/history/encyclopedias-almanacs.../fruit-mythology

Davidson, Alan, 1999, The Oxford Companion to Food, New York, NY, Oxford University Press Inc., p.757

Amidor, Toby, 2009, In Season: Strawberries, https://www.foodnetwork.com/healthyeats/in-season/2009/06/in-season-strawberries

**CITRON**

Kaufman, David, 1932, Poisons and Poisoning Among the Romans, Classical Philology, Vol. 27, pp.156-167, Penelope.uchicago.edu/Thayer/E/Journals/CP/27/2/Poisoning.*html

Gotefridi, Baroness Adelindus filia, 2016,Poison – Hmlock –art, Stefan's Florilegium, www.florilegium.org/?http%3A//www.florilegium. org/files/CRIME/Poison-Hmlock-art.html

Pliny the Elder, The Natural History, Book XXIII, The Remedies Derived from the Cultivated Trees, Chap. 56, www.perseus.tufts. edu/hopper/text?doc=Perseus%3Atext%3A1999.02.0137%3A-book%3D23%3Achapter%3D56

Geggel, Laura, 2017, Sour Note: In Ancient Rome, Lemons Were Only for the Rich, Live Science, https://www.livescience.com/59896-ancient-citrus-trade-routes.html

Adamson,Melitta Weiss (Ed), Segan, Francine (Ed), 2008, Entertaining From Ancient Rome to the Super Bowl: H – Z, Wesport, CT, Greenwood Press, Vol. 2, p. 420, https://books.google.com/ books?id=isbn-13: 978-0313339578, isbn -10:0313339570

Marienberg, Evyatar, 2011, The Stealing of the Apple of Eve from the 13th century Synagogue of Winchester, The Apple of Eve, Chapel Hill, NC, www.academia.edu/1481858/_The_Stealing_of_the_Apple_of_ Eve_from_the_13th_century_Synagogue_of_Winchester_

Sonneman, Toby, The Saga of the Citron, Reform Judaism.org, https://reformjudaism.org/Saga-Citron

Citron, radio Islam International, www.radioislam.org.za?a/index. php/library/162-signs-of-allah.html

Buddha's Hand citron, Citrus Variety Collection, University of California Riverside, College of Natural and Agricultural Sciences, https://citrusvariety.ucr.edu/citrus/buddha.html

Genetic analysis of citron (Citrus Medica L) using simple sequence repeats and single nucleotide polymorphisms, 2015, Scientia Horticulturae, Vol. 195, pp. 124-137, https://www. Sciencedirect.com/

science/article/pii/S0304423815301692?via%3Dihub

**RED CURRANTS**

The Viking Discovery of North America, 2011, Alan's Mysterious
World, https://alansmysteriousworld.wordpress.com/2011/08/18/
the-viking-discovery-of-north-america/

Growing Red Currants: Planting and Care (Moscow Region), vsadui-
doma.com/en/2018/11/25/vyrashhivanie-krasnoj-smorodiny-po-
sodka-i-uhod-moskovskaya-oblast

Davidson, Alan, 1999, The Oxford Companion to Food, New York,
NY, Oxford University Press Inc., p.235

FXCuisine, A Jam Fit For A Queen, fxcuuisine.com/default.asp?/lan-
guage=2&Display=213resolution=high

Something Sweet from Bar-le-Duc, https://www.groseille.com/en-
glish/something-sweet-from-bar-le-duc/

**RASPBERRY**

Friedman, Amy, Johnson, Meredith, 2004, The Raspberry King (A
Scandinavian Tale), https://www.uexpress.com/tell-me-a-sto-
ry/2004/8/29/the-raspberry-king-a-scandanavian-tale

Hunter, John P, 2014, Health Benefits From Food And Spices, Washington, DC, TX#PHIL.4-6-77-9HMC#LLCP, https://books.google.
com/books?id=TrMWBAAAQBAJ&pg=PA174&lpg=PA174&d-
q=health+benefits+from+foods+spices+john+hunter+raspberry&-
source=bl&ots=

Chippewa and Ojibwa Called the July Raspberry Moon, https://www.
edu/skywise/Indianmoons.html

Indians, Insanity, and American History Blog, Winter Food, cantonasylumfortheindians.com/history_blog/winterfood/

Hunter, Candace, 2008, Raspberry History, Folklore, Myth and Magic, https://www.thepracticalherbalist.com/holistic-medicine-library/raspberry-myth-and-magic

Randolph, Octavia,2014, In Pursuit of Beauty, Early Cosmetics, English History Authors, https://englishhistoryauthors.blogspot.com/2014/01/in-pursuit-of-beauty-early-cosmetics.html

The Free Dictionary by Farlex, https://www.thefreedictionary.com/Blowing+a+Raspberry

Davidson, Alan, 1999, The Oxford Companion to Food, New York, NY, Oxford University Press Inc., p.653

Raspberry Facts, www.softschools.com?facts/plants/raspberry_facts/1208/

**LEMON**

When Life Hands You Lemons, Make Lemonade, 2013, https://hermeticalhealth.me/2013/04/24/when-life-hands-you-lemons-make-lemonade/

Tree Magick, hafapea.com/magickpages/treemagick.html

Davidson, Alan, 1999, The Oxford Companion To Food, New York, NY, Oxford University Press Inc., p.449

Zak, Victoria, 2006, The Magic Teaspoon: Transform Your Meals With The Power of Healing Herbs and Spices, https://books.google.com/books?isbn+425209830

The History of Limonade, 2016, When Life Hands You Lemons, Make

Qatarzimat, https://recipereminiscing.wordpress.com/201607/06/
the-history-of-limonade-when-life-hands-you-lemons-make-qatar-
zimat

Food History Timeline, www.foodreference.com/html/html/
food-timeline-1676-1699.html

Le Coeur, Ursula, 2013, Hope In A Jar: Victorian Ladies Made Themselves Up, ursulalecoeur.com/hope-in-a-jar-victorian-ladies-made-
themselves-up/#sthash.Y9D.TomM.dpbs

Brunsel, P, 2004, Stonewall Jackson, a hypochondriac?, https://use-
lectionatlas.org/FORUM/index.php?topic=51660

**GRAPE**

Otto, Walter F., Palmer, Robert (T), 1965, Dionysus: Myth and Cult,
Bloomington, Indiana, Indiana University Press, https://philpapers.
org/rec/ADKWFO

Athenaeus of Naucratis, 2nd century AD, The Deipnosophists, Olson,
S. Douglas(T&Ed), 2010, Boston, MA, Harvard university Press, www.
hup.harvard.edu/catalog.php?isbn+9780674996397

Jones, Anita W, 2008, Healthy, Wealthy & Wise: A thorough and bal-
anced analysis of Biblical diet and wellness from Genesis to Revela-
tion, Xulon Press, page.97, https://books.google.ad/books?id=isbn
-978-1-60647-986-5

Jewish Treats: Juicy Bits of Judaism Daily, 2013, www.jewishtreats.
org/2013/04/which-tree-was-it.html

Filippone, Peggy Trowbridge, 2019, What Are Raisins? Raisin History, https://www.thespruceeats.com/raisins-history-and-over-
view-1807866

Albe, Sarah, Dog days of History: The Incredible Story of Our Best Friends, Washington, DC, National Geographic Books, P.76, https://books.google,com/books?id=WpFPDwAAQBAJ&pg=PA76+dg=-did+robert+peary+take+raisins+to++the+north+pole&souce

Asia Society, https://asiasociety.org/trade-silk-road-cities

Hirsch, Emil G., Eisenstein, Judah David,1906, Wine: The Jewish Encyclopedia, www.jewishencyclopedia.com/articles/14941-wine

Wine Symbolizes Blood – Bible Tools, https://www.bibletools.org/index.ctni/fusesection/.../wine-symbolizing blood.htm

## GOOSEBERRY

Rao, Subba, 2013, From the Donkey's Mouth and Other Short Stories, Bloomington, IN, XLIBRIS Corporation, p.79, ISBN 978-1-4836-4271-0, https://book.google.com/books/about/From_Donkey's_Mouth_and_Other_Short_Stor.htm/?id=7tMg6_4xFSoC

Gooseberry Facts: Soft Schools.com, www.softschools.com/facts/plants/gooseberry_facts/14541/
Experimental Psychology & Child Study: The New Educator's Library, 1922, London, UK, Sir Isaac Pitman & Sons, LTD., p.117, https://books.google.com/books?id=9hFVAAAAMAAJ&pg=PA117&dg=children+were+told+babies+came_from+from++q+gooseberry+bushes+source=bl&ots=

Slevin, Hugh, 1937, Cure for a Sty on the Eye, Dublin, IE, Dublin City University, https://www.duchas.ie/en/cbes/4605926/4603030/4644320

Ayto, John, The Diner's Dictionary: Word Origins of Food and Drink, 1993, Oxford, UK, Oxford University Press, p. 155, https://books.google.com/books?id=isbn -978-0-19-964024-9

Davidson, Alan, 1999, The Oxford Companion to Food, New York, NY, Oxford University Press Inc., p. 345

**BANANAS**

The Menehune, Also known as Nawao, mythicalrealm.com/creatures/menehunes.html

Kepler, Angela Kay, 1998, Hawaiian Heritage Plants, Honolulu, HI, University of Hawaii Press, p.25, ISBN-0-8248-1994-2, https://books.google.com/books?id=6DjyNkRevskC&printsec=frontcover&source=gbs.ge=summary_r&cad=0#v=onepage&q&f=false

Hastings, James (Ed), Selbie, John Alexander (Ed), Gray, Louis H. (Ed), 1916, Encyclopaedia of Religion and Ethics: Life and Death-Mulla, New York, NY, Charles Scribner's Sons, Vol. VIII, p.535, https://books.google.com/books?id=eEwTAAAAYAAJ&pg=PA535&lpg=PA535&dq=ancient+ulawa+people+beliefs&source
Kerrigan, Michael, 2015, Dark History of the Bible: The Sins, The Temptation, The Betrayal, and The Word, London, UK, Amber Books Ltd, https:books.google.com/books?id=isbn -978-1-78274-280-7

Destergers, Jake, 2014, Old Sea Superstitions and Nautical Terms, The Triton Nautical News For Captains and Crews, https://www.the-triton.com/2014/07/old-sea-superstitions-and-nautical-terms

History of Bananas – Where Did Bananas Originate?, www.tidalimpex.com/blog/history-of-bananas-where-did-bananas-originate/

Looby, Audrey, 2015, No Bananas On Boats, USC Digital Folklore Archives, folklore.usc.edu/?p=27091

Banana Trees Are Actually Giant Herbs-The Daily Meal, https://www.the dailymeal.com/cook/banana-trees-are-actually-giant-herbs

**APRICOT**

Mark, Joshua J., 2014, Megara, https://www.ancient.eu/Megara_

Krska, Boris, 2018, Genetic Apricot Resources and Their Utilisation in Breeding, https://www.intechopen.com/books/breeding-and-health-benefits-of-fruit-and-nut-crops/genetic-apricot-resources-and-their-utilisation-in-breeding

Nectar, Merriam-Webster, https://www.merriam-webster.com/dictionary/nectar

World Food and Wine, Apricot, https://world-food-and-wine.com/Apricot, New World Encyclopedia, www.newworldencyclopedia.org/entry/Apricot

Folklore Society Publication, 1892, German Christmas and the Christmas Tree, London, UK, David Nutt, Vol. 3, p.178, https://books.google.com/books?id=q1gCAAAAMAAJ&pg=PA179&1pg=PA179&dq=apricots+as+german+christmas+trees&source

USC Digital Folklore Archives, Don't Bring Apricots On A Tank, folklore.usc.edu/?p=29793

Davidson, Alan, 1999, The Oxford Companion To Food, New York, NY, Oxford University Inc., Press, p.25

Food In Space/National Air And Space Museum, https://airandspace.si.edu/exhibitions/apollo-to-the.../astronaut-life/food-in-space.cfm

**PLUM**

Kidd, Natalie, 2010,The Hidden History of Nursery Rhymes, https://www.education.com/magazine/articles/hidden_history_of_nursery_rhymes/

The Plum Blossom: A Symbol Of Strength – The Epoch Times, https://www.theepochtimes.com/the-plum-blossom-a-symbol-of-strength_1497107.html

Friday Harbor Holistic Health, www.fridayharborholistichealth.com/uncategorized/umeboshi-plums-for-good-health/

Jivong, Dong, 2011, Chang'an, city of fashion,www.chinadaily.com.cn/m/expo2011/2011-03/041content_12242336.htm
Food of the Samurai Period, https://www.saurai_archives.com/food.html/

Flowering Plum Trees, The Tree Center, https://www.thetreecenter.com/flowering-trees/flowering-plum-trees/

Prunus Americana, American Plum, https://sites.google.com/a/macalester.edu/ordwipedia/traditional-ecological-knowledge-tek-from-ling-2251/traditional-ecological-knowledge-tek-from-ling-2251/edible-knowledge/prunus-americana-americanplum?tmpl=...

Fryer, Janet, 2010, Prunus American, https://www.fs.fed.us/data_base/feis/plants/shrub/pruame/all.html

Amweiner, 2017, Civil War Talk, https://civilwartalk.com/threads/plums.135926/

ALL ABOUT PLUMS, www.samcooks.com/food/fruit/plums

**BLACKBERRY**

Alexander, Courtney, 2016, Berries As Symbols and In Folklore, Ithaca, NY, Department of Horticulture, Cornell University's College of Agriculture and Life Sciences, https://cpb-us-e1.wpmucdn.com/blogs.cornell.edu/dist/0/7265/files/2016/12.berryfolklore-2ljzt0q pdf

Colton, Stephen, 2017, Take On nature: the blackberry sprite – watch out, bogles about, Belfast, NIR, The Irish News, https://www.irish-news.com/lifestyle/2017/09/09/news/take-on-nature-the-blackberry-sprite-watch-out-bogles-about-1127865/

Haraldskaer Woman, Atlas Obscura, https://www.atlasobscura.com/places/haraldsk-r-woman

Locke, Tony, 2017, Tales of the Irish Hedgerow, Dublin, IE, The History Press Ireland, EPUB ISBN 978 0 7509 82993

Earle, Alice Morse, 1898, Stockbridge, MA, The Berkshire Traveller Press, https://www.gutenberg.org/files/22675/22675-h/22675-h.htm

Aloba, Arlissa, 2015, Fun Facts of Blackberries, Serving Joy, Inspire Through Sharing, servingjoy.com/fun-facts-of-blackberries

**ALMOND**

Demophon: Greek Mythology, https://www.greekmythology.com/Myths/Mortals/Demephon/demophon.html

Grieve, Margaret, A Modern Herbal, 1931, Mineola, NY, Dover Publications, Vol. I, p.22, ISBN – 13: 978 - 0 - 486 - 22798 -6, https://books.google.com/books?id=isbn -10:0-486-22798-7

National Almond Day! February 16, History of Amonds, www.nationalalmondday.com/history - of - almonds.html

Swenson, Allan A, 2008, Foods Jesus Ate And How To Grow Them, New York, NY, Skyhorse Publishing, https://books.goAQBAJ&pg=PT203&lpg=PT203&dq=The+rod+of+aaron+bore+sweet+almonds+on+one+side&source=bl&ots
Clarke, Jim, 2017, In The Middle Ages, The Upper Class went Nuts For Almond Milk, https://www.atlasobscura.com/articles/almond-milk-obsession-origins-middle-ages

Wilder, Emily, 2018, Bees for Hire: California Almonds Become Migratory Colonies' Biggest Task, https://weat.stanford.edu/news/blogs/and-the-west-blob/2018/bees-for-hire-california-almonds-now-are-migratory-colonies-biggest-task

**POMELO**

Chang'e Flying to the Moon: Chinese Mid-Autumn Festival Stories, https://www.chinesehighlights.com/festivals/mid-autumn-festi-val-story.htm

Why are Pomelo Fruits Eaten During Moon Festival?, https://asian-inspirations.com.au/Food-Knowledge/why-are-pomelo-fruits-eat-en-during-moon-festival/

Lee, Jonathan H. X. (Ed), Nadeau, Kathleen M (Ed), 2011, Encyclo-pedia of Asian Folklore and Folklife, Santa Barbara, Ca, ABC-CLIO, LLC, ISBN: 978-0-313-3

Yuzu Citrus From A To Z : 26 Things To Know, Saibante, Carolina Tra-verso, 2017, Fine Dining Lovers, https://www.finedininglovers.com/Stories/what-is-yuzu-citrus/

Davidson, Alan, 1999, Oxford Companion to Food, New York, NY, Oxford University Press Inc., p. 618

Mission Ramblings, celebrating Moon Festival, mustions-ramble-tai-wan.blogspot.com/2014/09/celebrating-moon-festival.html

**TOMATO**

Smith, Annabelle K, 2013, Smithsonian.com, https://www.smithso-nianmag.com/arts-cultural/why-the-tomato-was-feared-in-europe-for-more-than-200-years-863735/

Tomato & Health, Tomatoes in France, www.tomatoandhealth.com/index.php/en/article/story/spread_of_tomato

Leonard, Mae, 2019, An Irishwoman's Diary: Hot Tomatoes, The Irish Times, Dublin, IE, https://irishtimes.com/culture/heritage/an-irish-wona-s-sdiary-hot-tomatoes-1.1788759

Henry J. Heinz Biography: Success Story of Heinz Ketchup Empire, https://astrumpeople.com/henry-j-heinz-biography/

Nix v. Hedden, 149 U.S. 304, (1893), https://supreme.justia.com/cases/federal/us/149/304/

Mayyasi, The Food Industrial Complex, Priceonomics, https://priceonomics.com/the-food-industrial- complex/

Hafner, Josh, 2018, World's Biggest Food Fight: Thousands hurl tomatoes at Spain's Tomatina FestivaL. USA TODAY, https://www.usatoday.com/story/news/nation-now/2018/08/29/tomatina-festival-tomatoes-bunol-spain-big-food-fight/1134377002/

## HUCKLEBERRY

Richards, Rebecca T., Alexander, Susan J., 2006, A Social History of Wild Huckleberry Harvesting in the Pacific Northwest, Portland, OR, USDA Forest Service, Chapter 2, https://www.fs.fed.us/pnw/pubs/pnw_gtr657.pdf

Huckleberry Information and History: Huckleberry-Hucklberries, What's Cooking America, https://whatscookingamerica.net/History/HuckleberryHistory.htm

Scott, Sage, 2018, 9 Fun Facts About Huckleberries, the Unofficial State Fruit of Montana, Everyday Wanderer, https://everydaywanderer.com/huckleberries

McMillen, Nathan D, 2010, Pennsylvania's Oldest Citizen, pabook2. libraries.pus.edu/palitmap/Hucleberry.html

**APPLE**

Black, Susa Morgan, Tree Lore: Apple, https://www.druidry.org/library/trees/tree-love-apple

Timeless Myths, The Many Faces of Merlin, https://www.timelessmyths.com/arturian/merlin.html

Strom, Caleb, 2017, Avalon: A Real Island Obscured by Legend, or Just a Legendary Island?, https://www.ancient-origins.net/myths-legends/avalon-real-island-obscured-legend-or-just-legendary-island-007685

Daley, Jason, 2017, How the Silk Road Created the Modern Apple, Smithsonian.com, https://www.smithsonianmag.com/smart-news/how-silk-road-created-modern-apple-180964521/

Walker, Julian, 2013, Discovering Words in the Kitchen, Oxford, UK, Shire Publications Ltd., webttycho.umuc.edu/.../wqUGbqqPdy/2-9780747807766-discovering-words-in-the-kitchen

What's the Truth About...The Apple in the Garden of Eden? Jewish Action, https://jewishaction.com/religion/jewish-law/whats-Truth-apple-garden-eden

11 Ways Hard Cider Shaped American History, mentalfloss.com/article/59048?11-ways-hard-cider-shaped-american-history

The Real Johnny Appleseed Brought Apples-and Booze- To The American Frontier, Smithsonian.com, https://www.smithsonianmag.com/arts-culture/real-johnny-appleseed-brought-applesand-booze-american-frontier-1809532631/

Apples and More, University of Illinois Extension.com, https://extension.illinois.edu/apples/facts.cfm

**WATERMELON**

Oklahoma Ag in the Classroom: Watermelon Facts, aitc.okstate.edu/lessons/extrafacts/melon.html

Watermelon Faith, www.1stpres.cc/wp-content/uploads/2012/03/watermelon-faith-1.pdf

Rogov, Daniel, 2002, Watermelon Days Are Here! HAARETZ, Israel, https://www.haaretz.com/food/1.5221646

Ling, Wan Yan, 2008, Snapshots from Asia: Watermelon Seed Cracker...'Just Wack,' Serious Eats, https://www.seriouseats.com/2008/01/snapshots-from-asia-watermelon-seed-cracker.html

Dee, Jane E, 1998, Art Teacher's Collection Rooted in Tradition, Hartford, CT, The Hartford Courant, https://www.courant.com/news/connecticut/hc-xpm-1996-03-12-9603120195-story.html

Chiffolo, Anthony F, Hesse, Rayner W., 2006, Cooking With The Bible, BIBLICAL FOOD, FEASTS, AND LORE, Westport, CT, https://books.google.com/books?id=isbn -10: 0-313-33410-2, isbn -13: 978-0-313-37561-3

**MULBERRY**

Pyramus and Thisbe Summary, www.supersummary.com/pyramus-and-thisbe/summary/

24 Fun and Fascinating Facts About Mulberries, 2018, tonsoffacts.com/24-Fun-and-Fascinating-Facts-about-Mulberries/

Rowland, Teisha, 2010, Turning Leaves Into Silk, Santa Barbara,

CA, Santa Barbara Independent, https://www.independent.com/news/2010/mar/12/turning-leaves-silk/

Coles, Peter, 2016, A Brief History of London's Mulberries, Spital-fields Life, spitalfieldslife.com/2016/06/29/a-brief-history-of-londons-mulberries/

Wiencek, Henry, 2012, Master of the Mountain: Thomas Jefferson and His Slaves, New York, NY, Farrar Straus and Giroux, p.34, ISBN 978-0-374-29956-9, https://www.publishersweekly.com/978-0-374-29956-9

Popular Science News, 1900, Vol. 34, p.23, New York, NY, Lillard & Company

**PINEAPPLE**

Levins, Hoag, Social History of the Pineapple: Being the Brief and Colorful Story of a Trully American Plant, levins.com/pineapple.htm/

Drew, Bonnie, 2012, Christopher Columbus Discovered Pineapples, Beaufort online, www.beaufortonline.com/christopher-colum-bus-discoveredpineapples/

The Story of the Pineapple, A Symbol of Hospitality & Warmth, 2013, Coastal Style Living Blog. www.beachdecorshop.com/blog/the-story-of-the-pineapple-a-symbol-of-hospitality-warmth/

Serda, Chef Clyde, the Story of the Pineapple, a Symbol of Hos-pitality, chefsblade.monster.com/news/articles/884-the-story-of-the-pineapple-a-symbol-of-hospitality

**ORANGE**

Skinner, F. (Ed), Finch, Myron (Ed), 1852, The Plough, The

Loom, and The Anvil, Philadelphia, PA, Published by Myron Finch, Volume 4, pp. 111, 112, https://books.google.com/books?id=imY4AQAAMAAJ&pg=PA111&lpg=PA111&pg=PA111&dq=the+plough,+the+loom+the+anvil,+a+venerable+orange+tree&spurce=blots=A_-Fbol0oB&sig=AcfU3

War of the Oranges, Iberian History, Encyclopaedia Britannica, httsp://www.britannica.com/event/War-of-the-Oranges

Royal Collection Trust, Headdress from the orange blossom parure 1846, https://www.rct.uk/collection/65305/headdress-from-the-orange-blossom-parure

Spellman, Tom, 2002. California's Second Great Gold Rush, Highland Area Historical Society, https://www.highlandhistory.org/California%20Second%20Great%20Gold%20Rush.php

Fallows, Deborah, 2015, California's Improbable Navel-Orange Queen, The Atlantic, https://www.theatlantic.com/national/archive/2015/05/california-navel-orange-queen/392624/

**CRANBERRY**

Native Languages of the Americas: Lenape/Delaware Indian Legends and Stories, Yakwawi: Lenape legend about a battle with the mastodons, www.native-languages.org/lenape-legends.htm

Wampanoag Tribe of Gay Head, www.wampanoagtribe.net/pages/wampanoag_way/other

The Cranberry Through Time, Understanding Cranberries, Cape Cod Cranberry Growers' Association, https://www.cranberries.org/exploringcranberries/into/av/cran_through_time.pdf

Sexton, Julia, 2010, Thanksgiving, The Civil war, and Cranberry Sauce, Westchester Co., www.westchestermagazine.com/

Westchester-Magazine/November-2010/Thanksgiving-The-Civil-War-And-Cranberry...

Cranberries Weren't Always Cranberries. Ocean Spray, https://www.oceanspray.com/en/Out-Story?About-the-Cranberry

Making Sense of Cranberries, A multisensory look at the properties of cranberries and cranberry products, www.cranberries.org/exploringcranberries/into/making_sense_cran.pdf

Davidson, Alan, 1999, The Oxford Companion To Food, New York, NY, Oxford University Press Inc, p. 223

Perry, Leonard, Cranberries For Thanksgiving, Burlington, VT, Department of Plant and Soil Service, https://pss.uvm.edu/ppp/articles/cranberry.html

The Cranberry Story, nj.gov/pinelands/infor/educational/curriculum/pinecur/tcs.htm

**PUMPKIN**

Hertz, Kayla, 2018, Original Jack-o-Lanterns Were Truly Terrifying and Made of Turnips, Irish Central, https://www.irishcentral.com/roots/history/original-irish-jack-o-lanterns-halloween-turnip

Theobald, Mary Miley, 2009, Some Pumpkins! Halloween and Pumpkins in Colonial America, Colonial Williamsburg Federation (US), https://www.history.ord/Foundation/journal/autumn09/pumpkins.cfm

Tuckman, Marilyn Alice, 2014, For the Love of Pumpkins: A Cookbook, Pittsburg, PA, Dorrance Publishing Company, https://books.google.com/books?id=Jx8OBAAAQBAJ&pg=PRll&dq=pilgrims+sliced+off+pumpkin+tops+filled+the+inside+with+milk+honey+and+spices&source

Johnson, J, 2017, Nothing Says Fall Like Pumpkins, University of Florida, UF/IFAS, Blogs, blogs.lFas.ufl.edu/lafayettco/2017/10/17/nothing-says-fall-like-pumpkins/

Pumpkin Facts, History, https://www.history.com/topics/halloween/pumpkin-facts

**EGGPLANT**

Andrews, Tamra, 2000, Nectar and Ambrosia: An Encyclopedia of Food in World Mythology, Santa Barbara, CA, ABC-CLIO, p.85

Botham, Noel, 2009,The World's Greatest Book of Useless Information, New York, NY, The Penguin Group, https://books.google.com/books?id=isbn -978-1-101-06135-0

Davidson, Alan, 1999, The Oxford Companion to Food, New York, NY, Oxford University Press Inc.

Trujillo, Linda, The Elegant Eggplant, Phoenix, AZ, Cooperative Extension Maricopa County Journal, https://cals.arizona.edu/maricopa/gaarden/html/pubs/0203/eggplant.html

Rupp, Rebecca, 2011, How Carrots Won The Trojan War: Curious (but true) Stories of Common Vegetables, North Adams, MA, Storey Publishing, ISBN 978-1-60342-968-9, https://books.google.com/books?id=Sl7lgyziGyoC&pg=PA155

Vogel, Mark R., 2008, Eggplant: A Botanical Identity Crisis, FoodReference.com,www.foodreference.com/html/arteggplant.html

Van Hare, Holly (Ed), 2017, Eggplant Contains Nicotine, But is it Addictive?, The Daily Meal, https://www.thedailymeal.com/healthy-eating/eggplant-contains-nicotine-it-addictive

# TOBACCO

Mooney, James, 1900, History, Myths, and Sacred Formulas of the Cherokee, Washington, DC, Published by the Bureau of American Ethnology, p.254
https://www.gutenberg.org/files/24788/24788-h/24788-h.htm

Winter, Joseph C. (Ed), 2000, Tobacco use by Native North Americans: Sacred Smoke and Silent Killer, Norman, OK, University of Oklahoma Press, p.324
https://books.google.com/books/about/Tobacco_Use_by_Native_North_Americans.html?id=UGl4hxx6mTQC, ISBN 0-8061-3262-0

The Long Tobacco Road: A History of Smoking from Ritual to Cigarette, randomhistory.com/2009/01/31_tobacco.html

Wexler, Thomas A., 2006, Tobacco: From Miracle Cure to Toxin, New Haven, CT, YaleGlobal Online, https://yaleglobal.yale.edu/tobacco-miracle-cure-toxin

Eisenfeld, Sue, 2014, Breaks in the Action, New York, NY, Opinionator, The New York Times, https://opinionator.blogs.nytimes.com/2014/02/07breaks-in-the-action/

Trueman, Shanon, 2019, The Botany of the Tobacco Plant, ThoughtCo, https://www.thoughtco.com/the-botany-of-the-tobacco-plant-419203